Arbortext for Authoring: An Author's Guide to Getting Started with Arbortext Editor

An Arbortext Monster Garage Book

JANICE SUMMERS

Copyright ©2022, *Single-Sourcing Solutions, Inc.*

All rights reserved. No part of this publication may be reproduced, stored in a retrieval system, or transmitted, in any form, or by any means, electronic, mechanical, photocopying, recording, or otherwise, without the prior consent of the publisher. Making or distributing electronic copies of this book constitutes copyright infringement and could subject the infringer to criminal and civil liability.

Although every precaution has been taken to verify the accuracy of the information contained herein, the author and publisher assume no responsibility for any errors or omissions. No liability is assumed for damages that may result from the use of the information contained within.

SECOND EDITION

Edited by: Liz Fraley

Published by: Single-Sourcing Solutions

PO Box 62122, Sunnyvale, CA 94089.

www.single-sourcing.com

info@single-sourcing.com

twitter.com/SingleSourcing

TC Dojo and Arbortext Monster Garage name and logos are the property of Single-Sourcing Solutions, Inc.

Arbortext product names and logos are the property of PTC Inc., ptc.com

ISBN: 978–1–7326766–4–0

Second edition: 2022. Updated for Arbortext 8.1

First edition: 2019

This book was written in DITA using Arbortext Editor and published for print, PDF, ePub, and MOBI using Arbortext Styler.

Arbortext Monster Garage Books

Arbortext for Authoring: An Author's Guide to Getting Started with Arbortext Editor

Arbortext 101: Best Practices for Configuring, Authoring, Styling, and Publishing with Arbortext

Arbortext 102: Best Practices for Creating Arbortext Styler Stylesheets

TC Dojo Books

Adding Custom Actions to OxygenXML Frameworks

For all of you who have been pushed into the deep end of the pool, I hope this book is the life preserver that will get you safely to where you need to be—authoring in Arbortext Editor with confidence and ease.

Contents

List of Figures xi
List of Tables xv
Chapter 1. Introduction 1
    Acknowledgement 2
    About the Author 3
    Installing Arbortext 3
Chapter 2. Leveling the authoring field 5
    Structured authoring in a nutshell 5
    What is a document type? 8
    Markup language 11
    The Arbortext suite of products 13
Chapter 3. You may know more than you realize 23
    Set up a local playground 25
Chapter 4. Getting familiar with Arbortext Editor 27
    Opening Arbortext Editor 28
    Opening a new sample file 29
    Using the split window screen 30
    Viewing markup 31
    Setting screen preferences 33
    Setting up your view 34
Chapter 5. Well-formed and valid documents 37
    Create a well-formed document 38
    Create a valid document 45
    Change or delete markup 51
    Move an element 53
    Expand and collapse 56
    Inserting comments 59
Chapter 6. Authoring your first document 61
    Build your foundation 64
    Adding text to your document 67
    Adding graphics 69
    Creating Tables 73

Fun with Tag Templates...79
Publishing in Arbortext 82
Cross-referencing...85
Chapter 7.   Authoring your first DITA document in Arbortext
        Editor 89
    DITA in 30 seconds..89
    All work starts with a plan 91
    The Resource Manager 93
    The DITA Map 97
    Create a DITA Map and then fill it in 98
        Authoring your topics 101
    Special options in DITA 103
Chapter 8.   Best practices for all authors 109
Chapter 9.   Top Arbortext and authoring resources.............113
Index..117

List of Figures

Figure 1.	Procedural vs. Descriptive	7
Figure 2.	Arbortext end-to-end solution suite	16
Figure 3.	Arbortext Editor screen shot	17
Figure 4.	IsoDraw for technical illustrations screen shot	17
Figure 5.	Creo Illustrate	18
Figure 6.	Styler	19
Figure 7.	Publish from the Editor window	21
Figure 8.	Windchill's web-based interface	22
Figure 9.	Insert graphic using toolbar icon	28
Figure 10.	Insert graphic using menu item	29
Figure 11.	Open a new sample file	30
Figure 12.	Changing the window view	31
Figure 13.	Change the tag display	32
Figure 14.	Show partial tags	33
Figure 15.	Setting up user preferences	34
Figure 16.	Increase or decrease the font size	35
Figure 17.	Create new Free-form document	39
Figure 18.	Assign Top Level Element tag	39
Figure 19.	Ways to pull up the Markup list	40
Figure 20.	Make up your own markup	41
Figure 21.	Sample of well-formed markup	42
Figure 22.	Finding the Publish menu item	43
Figure 23.	Publish window	44
Figure 24.	With no DTD, there is no formatting	45
Figure 25.	Open a new DocBook template	46
Figure 26.	DocBook template with some basic markup	47
Figure 27.	Four ways to open the Insert Markup options list	48
Figure 28.	Sample out-of-the-box Styler DocBook	50
Figure 29.	Sample well-formed and valid DocBook markup	51

Arbortext for Authoring

Figure 30.	Change Markup	53
Figure 31.	Move selected content to a new location	54
Figure 32.	New chapter order	56
Figure 33.	Collapse areas of the document	57
Figure 34.	Hiding graphics from view	59
Figure 35.	Insert comments	60
Figure 36.	Gathering the pieces for authoring	63
Figure 37.	Opening a new DocBook file	65
Figure 38.	Start to build an empty shell	66
Figure 39.	The beginning of my book on lavender	67
Figure 40.	Modify the graphic attributes	71
Figure 41.	Graphic size is modified	72
Figure 42.	Hiding graphics will give you a cleaner workspace	73
Figure 43.	You can use Table or Informaltable. Switching is easy.	74
Figure 44.	Table tools	75
Figure 45.	Table width attribute	78
Figure 46.	Modify Attributes from the Document Map or the Edit Window	79
Figure 47.	Opening Tag Templates	80
Figure 48.	Name the Tag Template	81
Figure 49.	Tag Template ready to fill in	82
Figure 50.	Request to publish	83
Figure 51.	Set the Save As location and pick the style sheet	84
Figure 52.	Side by side view of published output and markup	85
Figure 53.	Create an ID	86
Figure 54.	Create ID's for many element types	87
Figure 55.	Content mapped to DITA structure	93
Figure 56.	Resource Manager and Topic management	95
Figure 57.	Resource Manager and Image management	96

Figure 58.	Map for generic collections and BookMap for books	98
Figure 59.	Create the New Topic	99
Figure 60.	My DITA Map example	101
Figure 61.	Opening topics	102
Figure 62.	Sample Published page	103
Figure 63.	Parts of the lavender bud	106

List of Tables

Table 1.	Handy shortcuts we all use	23
Table 2.	Going beyond the basics	24
Table 3.	Now I have a numbered table	105

Chapter 1.   Introduction

Topics Covered in this Chapter
- Acknowledgement
- About the Author
- Installing Arbortext

If you find yourself in a situation where you need to learn Arbortext and you need to do it fast, then this book was written for you.

The goal was to create a guidebook that could serve a large audience from authors who are veteran writers who only need to learn a new tool to writers who may be new to the field of technical authoring. Both need the same thing: an effective way to learn Arbortext Editor.

By following the exercises laid out for you in this book, I believe that you'll be authoring with confidence in no time. Arbortext tools really are easy to use once you master the basics.

This book is based on Single-Sourcing Solutions's years of being Arbortext specialists and our decades of mentoring, coaching, and training others. Over the years we have fielded countless calls from many who started out where you may be, new to the tool, new to structured authoring, and new to DITA. Some have been eager and willing learners, and some have had to overcome a bit of resistance. I am very proud to say that all of them have journeyed through our mentoring and have become masters and teachers themselves.

I am not going to cover every feature in Arbortext; that would take too long and it's not necessary. Arbortext comes with a detailed help section and even some productive practice lessons. I'm simply going to cover enough to get you started and help you complete one simple document start to finish.

There are many methods to learning. Some do well jumping into the deep end and others like to get their toes wet first. Personally, I prefer to master the basics and then jump in and experiment. With a solid foundation you can always find your footing. There is a reason the first lesson you learn in swimming after how to float is how to tread water. No matter what happens in the water, if you can tread water, you can save yourself.

In this book, we are going to do several exercises together. I will share my examples so you can compare them with your work. At the end of an exercise look for **Here is what I have**. Although it doesn't replace me being there with you, I hope it helps deepen the learning experience for you. Nothing can ever replace being face to face or at least voice to voice. We prefer the richness of active dialog because it allows us to customize the training to suit the learner. You can ask questions and get immediate and direct responses. It is not possible to do that in a book. Of course, if you ever need us, you can always call us!

This book is meant to be an introduction and not a replacement for more detailed in-depth learning. Nor is it meant to replace the wonderful help inside the Arbortext tools and the free eLearning library you have access to. You should take advantage of all the resources available for you to learn from. With a solid foundation and basic mastery of the tool, you can expand to more advanced skills.

Acknowledgement

Special thanks to Elizabeth Fraley for constantly pushing me into the deep end of the pool! I have known her for many years and have had the privilege to work closely with her for well over a decade now. The life lessons I have gained are immeasurable, but the most important ones have been in treading water with confidence. This is analogous to the world of Tech Comm where she proceeded to push me into the water. It was up to me to learn how to keep my head above water and propel myself forward. Of course she would never let me drown she knew the value of me learning to find my way.

I am very fortunate to have someone in my corner who has my back through all the highs and lows, peaks, and valleys. Special thanks to Roger Thompson. There is a great deal more I could say here, but there is no need because I tell him every day.

Thank you so much Single-Sourcing Solutions's customers who have trusted us to help guide you. I can speak for all of us when I say we feel very fortunate to have such wonderful customers who we genuinely enjoy spending time with. It is a privilege and a delight to serve you.

About the Author

I fell into this field rather accidentally over a decade ago. You could say I stumbled into the deep end of the pool and had to learn how to tread fast. While I had the good fortune to work with one of the most knowledgeable people in the industry, there was no time to hold my hand and gently mentor my growth. Business demanded that I jump in and figure it out.

Since I did not come from a Tech Comm background I had to learn the lingo while learning a whole new tool suite. Lucky for me, I landed in Single-Sourcing Solutions and the driving force behind the company is to do and teach. It is a rare perspective for a consulting company to be so dedicated to open sharing of lessons learned, and I believe that has made all the difference for me. I know it does for our customers.

Looking back, I'm glad for the entry path I had. While it may have been rough, and I had moments of panic, I have always had a life raft. I hope this book will be a life raft for you, a foundation to help you tread water and float.

Installing Arbortext

I'm assuming you are reading this because you need to use Arbortext.

Arbortext for Authoring

While it's not a requirement, having Arbortext installed would make the exercises more meaningful. Even if you are "Arbortext Curious" and you aren't sure about committing to a single subscription, you might want to have at least a trial version as you walk through this book.

Make sure you are able to publish as well before you proceed. While frequent publishing is discouraged under normal conditions, you will want to see the effects of authoring with markup as you execute the exercises. Once you are comfortable with how structured authoring works in Arbortext, you will only push to publish when you absolutely need to. With Arbortext we learn to trust the outcome as long as our markup is correct. We are liberated from the page and we can focus on what really matters—the content.

If you need help with accessing, acquiring, installing, and configuring any of the Arbortext products, you can reach out to us here at Single-Sourcing Solutions or you can purchase our *Arbortext 101* book. *Arbortext 101* goes above the standard out-of-the box installation by covering customized configurations, making it a key resource for any Arbortext owner.

Chapter 2. Leveling the authoring field

Topics Covered in this Chapter
- Structured authoring in a nutshell
- What is a document type?
- Markup language
- The Arbortext suite of products

Many people like me found their way into Technical Communication from a non-traditional path. If you are among them, don't worry you have landed in the right place. I have included some foundation information about structured authoring to get you up to speed.

Perhaps you are not new to structured authoring, but you need to learn the tool navigation. Just skip the portions of the book that you don't feel would offer any value for you personally.

Structured authoring in a nutshell

Structured authoring is the process of marking up content that gives the various pieces a structural meaning according to a schema.

The biggest motivation to shift to a structured authoring model is money. Reducing cost while increasing revenue is the driving force for any company and technical publications plays a crucial role. Clear, concise, and accurate customer-facing information is often a key differentiation in customer purchases and adoption.

There are many more benefits, but these are the top three reasons:

- **Consistency**—All authors conform to the same way of doing things. No need to fix formatting issues; the style is enforced through Styler and not the authoring interface.

Arbortext for Authoring

- **Centralize & Automate**—Create reusable components, assemble compositions based on profiles or output types. This is also where you can experience a huge benefit if you need to localize your content. Just send out the bits and receive them back to be automatically inserted when and where they need to be.
- **Future Proofing your content**—In Arbortext, the content is human readable as it is created using industry standard XML/SGML. Any tool that can read XML can open an Arbortext file. Arbortext is standards based, pure and simple.

How does it work?

Structured authoring is a way of adding background codes that indicate what is coming so the information can be presented in a predefined way. Think of one machine talking to another machine defining what is coming and explaining what to do with it, how to treat it, and how to display it. Structured authoring allows us to free the information from the page by automating formatting so that authors can focus on what really matters—the content. Structured authoring also has mechanisms to automatically insert smaller content pieces like short legal disclaimers, company branding/messaging, health and safety tips, corporate address, etc.

Desktop publishing is procedural and is preoccupied with how the published output will look. With desktop publishing you set the font family, size, color, and any other attribute on each occurrence. Thus, the style is hard coded to the content. Take Title for example. Titles can appear in many places; the chapter level, the section level, on a table, on a figure, etc. So, with the Title, you would need to specify the final style at each occurrence. With structured authoring you only need to specify Title, and the formatting of the Title is conditioned on the location inside the document.

Another important difference to note with desktop publishing tools is that what you see on the screen is what you will see in the output

(WYSIWYG). With unstructured content the formatting is hard coded to the content. It is *procedural* while structured authoring is *descriptive*. Consider the Title we just mentioned. In structured authoring we describe what is coming next—Title—and we allow automation to format the Title based on where it is in the document. Is the Title in a chapter, a graphic, a table, a section?

Figure 1. Procedural vs. Descriptive

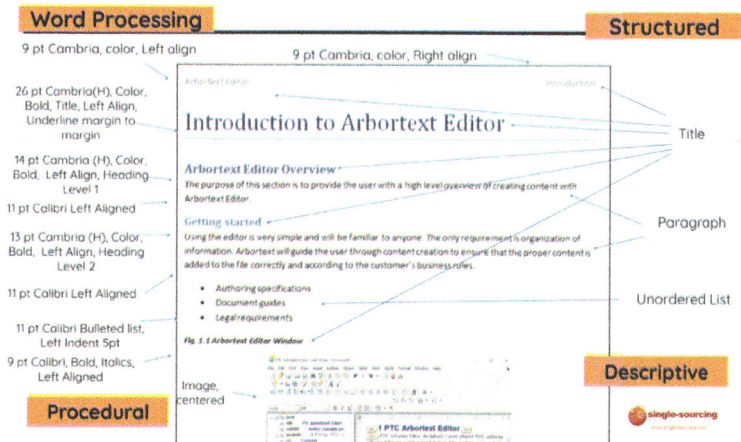

With structured authoring, the focus switches to what the *purpose* of the content is, what role it plays in the greater document. When you author in Arbortext, you simply assign the <title> tag. The same tag is applied to any and every title and how that information is formatted and displayed is influenced by the context; where the title is in the document and what type of output is being generated (web, print, in application....). There is no need to consider the formatting for each type of title; this is handled in composition. The only thing the author needs to know is that the content is a title and it has been given the <title> tag and that it is used in proper context.

In structured authoring what you see on the screen is merely one representation. We say it is one possibility. It is not what the finished output will look like since the structured document can be output to many output types. As an author, your role ends with making sure you have used the correct descriptive markup (tag) as you write. This is the biggest shift for most people: Letting go of "What you see is what you get." Once they do, they feel liberated.

What is a document type?

The document type defines how to shape and manage the content and what markup you can use to help define the content.

There are several forms of structure or architectural styles and it is important to know which one you are authoring in because each one has it's own set of rules. And, when it comes to XML, the extensible nature of the markup means that the mark up or tags may also be unique to the document type. In the exercises that follow, you will see the role of the DTD (Document Type Definition) and how you can select which one to author to. Arbortext can use any well-constructed DTD or XSD (XML Schema Definition) schema. It doesn't care; it supports SGML and XML natively and has since its inception. In fact, Arbortext was designed to support custom doctypes from the very first release. This means it can support any architecture you can imagine now and into the future.

DocBook

In my opinion, this is the easiest architecture to learn. Its linear, traditional book-type design comes as second nature. The architecture is structurally broad, with elements that further define smaller pieces of the full document. It starts at the highest level and narrows down to define the smaller pieces. While you could take a modular approach in creating the documents, it's not necessary. This document structure is fine, if not preferred, for publications that are written once and never changed, like articles. The language is either SGML or XML.

DITA

DITA (Darwin Information Typing Architecture) was designed and developed by IBM and they used Arbortext Editor to do it. DITA depends on a modular approach to authoring. All content conforms to specific topic types and is authored to stand alone or be seamlessly inserted into a larger publication. While out of the box DITA has a handful of topic types it also allows for specialization. Specialization means you can create your own topic types to fit your needs. For example, the DITA training topic types have a full set specialization for content creators who write for training purposes. A finished document is built with a series of independently written topics pulled together with a map. Those who author in DITA also tend to have a strong drive to maximize reuse and take a minimalist approach to writing. If you are serious about DITA then I strongly encourage you to get very familiar with what minimalism is and how to apply it to the information you create. For reuse, there is no replacement for taking the time to do an analysis of all of the documentation you or your team supports for the organization. DITA source documents are XML and DITA produced by Arbortext is XML.

I may be biased here but I believe DITA is much easier in the long run. When I had started out in Technical Communication, I was in MIL-SPEC (Military Specification). Then I transitioned to DocBook for commercial projects which was pretty similar to MIL-SPEC; its just easier markup. Then I was thrust into DITA and once I got through the initial phase it became the easiest architecture to use. It just requires discipline.

I first started to write this book in DocBook. After all, this is a book. I wasn't concerned with reuse which is one of the biggest drives for people to move into DITA. I wanted to be a bit lazy so I knew I could work in DocBook. I could still write in the modular spirit of DITA without topic types and I could have a loose plan.

That worked fine for the first two chapters. After that, I began to feel frustrated with the limits in DocBook, so I moved the entire book over to DITA.

MIL-STD and Defense

There are several large military standards, MIL-STD-38784, MIL-STD-40051, MIL-STD-3001, S1000D to name a few. Each one has its own set of rules and specific markup and the specs are very detailed and complex. With Arbortext Editor, you can author in any one of these specifications. Historically, Arbortext Editor has been the preferred tool for authoring content for this industry probably because Arbortext Editor is very robust and can perform under any specification. The language can be either SGML or XML. The DTD — the part that governs how you author—is owned and managed by the government agency so all you need to do is receive the DTD for your specific contract. Install this in your custom directory and author away. Yes, it's that simple and yet complicated. Remember the DTD? All DTDs are not the same. There is no "one DTD fits all" in defense, so be aware.

Other document types

There are other document architectures, like the ATA standard, that are less common. You may even find yourself in the rare situation where a company has developed its own. This is not a recommended approach as it can turn into a nightmare to manage. The closer you are to the generally accepted standard the more cost effective your technical publications will be.

But if you are in this situation, the good news is that Arbortext was designed to support custom doctypes from the start so it will have no problem supporting anything you encounter or create.

Markup language

Markup is the shorthand to structure. Originally designed to enable the sharing of machine-readable large-project documents in government, law, and industry, it continues to evolve over time.

Developed and standardized in the 1960s, Structured Generalized Markup Language, or SGML, was the first version of markup language to be widely accepted. While it's still in use today, usually you only find it in legacy documentation. XML evolved from SGML and dominates the scene today. Like its parent SGML, XML is descriptive and uses tags, but it is easier to learn because the emphasis is on simplicity. You could say it was developed from lessons learned with SGML.

The magic of markup is made up of three pieces—Elements, Attributes, and Entities. Let's briefly cover each one.

Again, my intent is not to go to deep here. I just wan to give you enough to get you going. It is important that you grasp the fundamental difference and the role each one plays. You can check out the Single-Sourcing Solutions's resources page if you want additional information.

Elements

Elements are the *name* of the content that follows. Think of it as the herald describing what is coming up. The description is held inside angle brackets `<address>` and is followed by a closing `</address>`.

Some common Elements

> Table—`<table>`
>
> Figure—`<figure>`
>
> Title—`<title>`

Arbortext for Authoring

> Section—`<section>`
>
> Example—`<example>`
>
> Note—`<note>`

Attributes

Attributes define a property of an element and you can have more than one attribute assigned to the element. The syntax always consists of a name-value pair that appears within the element's start tag. For example `<element-name attribute1, attribute2, ...> element content</element-name>`.

Attributes can affect formatting or define property

> A graphic element `<graphic fileref="images/34RT567.pdf">` image goes here`</graphic>`
>
> A title element `<title id="boatSystems-6A30B3EF">` title text goes here `</title>`
>
> A note element `<note type-"danger">` content goes here`</note>`

Entities

An entity is the mechanism that allows you to define replacement values. The name is declared in the entity along with the value. When the name is later called inside the document the declared value is inserted.

Company Name Example

Declared: `<!ENTITY sample1 "My Company Name">`

Called: `We all work at` **`&sample1;`** `in New York`

Published reads: We all work at **My Company Name** in New York

Some other examples

Copyright owner: `<!ENTITY copyright "Copyright W3Schools">`

Called: `&copyright;`

Published reads: **Copyright W3Schools**

A writer's name: `<!ENTITY writer "Donald Duck">`

Called: `The author of this book is &writer;`

Published reads: The author of this book is **Donald Duck**

The Arbortext suite of products

The Arbortext Technical Communication solution is a full suite of products that cover every aspect from authoring through composing to management and omnichannel delivery. The suite is part of a larger enterprise solution set owned by PTC. At Single-Sourcing Solutions, we are avid users, implementers, and trainers of the tool suite.

Arbortext is not the only solution we know. In fact, it is not the only solution we have recommend to writing teams. There are times when Arbortext is not the right solution. We have always been candid about those situations when we consult with our clients. Deciding on a tool should be an exercise you go into after you analyze several factors that have nothing to do with tools at all.

There are a few good reasons why we tend to like Arbortext as a solution for content creation, management, and delivery and why we like to use it. Here are my top five reasons.

The first is that Arbortext is a robust end-to-end solution with pieces that cover every part of the content life cycle. We prefer a solution that works well together without having the added frustration and cost of building bridges between multiple vendor solutions. If anything goes wrong you can make one call. There is no finger pointing to other vendors. Plus, when updates happen—and updates always happen

Arbortext for Authoring

—you can be assured that the solution has been vetted with all the other pieces together, so it works out of the box.

The second reason is that it is a suite of parts that are designed to work together but you do not have to get every part to get going. In fact, we have long-time customers who only have parts of the suite. A decade later they are still doing just fine with the pieces they purchased out of the gate. We even have clients with one-person writing teams that only have a couple of pieces and they get on just fine. Just because you are a small and mighty team doesn't mean you don't deserve the best tools! In fact, I have found the opposite to be true. Small teams with limited resources need the most out of their tools. With Arbortext you get that. And you can get what you need for now and add parts as you go.

If you have ever worked in a controlled, audited, or geographically diverse team environment then you will understand the third reason all too well. There is a way to comment on your content in the authoring stage to communicate special instructions or necessary information inside the source file that will not affect the published output. Even in a team of one this is handy since you can make a comment for future reference as well. No need to try and remember why you did what you did, write it down. With the content management piece, you get revision control and an irrefutable audit trail of historical information. It will let you track what was done, why it was done, and who approved it.

I like tools I can use now and 20 years from now. Longevity is the fourth reason I like Arbortext as a solution of choice. At the writing of this book, I believe Arbortext Editor is now 30+ years old. It did not start out as Arbortext; it started as Epic Editor. PTC has continued to evolve the product and build out the suite of tools to keep pace with the demands of today's requirements. Who knew 30 years ago that IVR (Integrated Virtual Reality) would be a "thing," yet here we are. The name may have changed a bit and the user interface has evolved —and there are some very handy new features—but it is still that dependable and reliable tool it always has been and will continue to be.

The fifth reason is probably the strongest one for me and it has to do with capability. I was fortunate to be raised in a family with artists and not a lot of money. Some of my favorite outings were our made-up picnics where we would drive to a field or a stand of trees or some other outdoor destination and eat our lunch. Each person had their own bit of paper and we shared sets of colored charcoal pencils. My mother, a very talented artist, would offer some basic advisory instruction but the rest was up to us to create. We decided what to draw and how to draw it with the colors we selected. That simple lesson has stayed with me all my life: When you work with the tools you need you can do anything. The Arbortext solution suite has all the capability you could ever want or need. There are some out-of-the-box templates you can use to get you started or for inspiration. It is like being handed a blank piece of paper and a box of colored pencils.

Arbortext may seem intimidating from the outside, but it really isn't when you get the hang of it, and anyone can get the hang of it with the right mentoring. You can do anything you want to do with Arbortext, and it can handle just about any challenge you want to throw at it. It can even handle the simple stuff.

You can always find up to date and detailed information on the Single-Sourcing Solutions website or on the PTC Arbortext site.

Arbortext for Authoring

Figure 2. Arbortext end-to-end solution suite

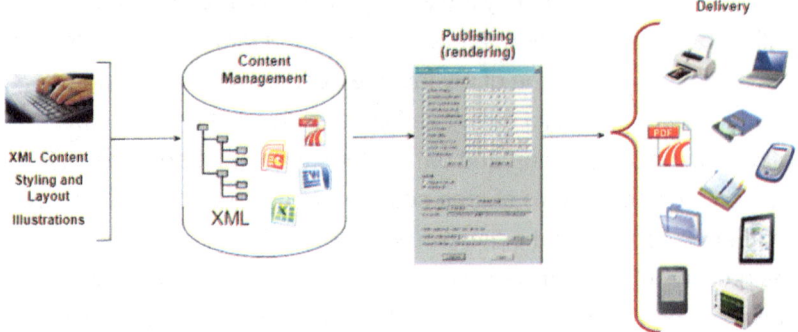

Authoring

As an author creating reusable, structured content, you will spend most of your time with PTC's Arbortext Editor which this is the focus for this book. Earlier I mentioned that Arbortext Editor has been around for 30 years so it's understandable that it is the industry's most adopted XML authoring tool. It's steady, stable, and reliable. Since it is native XML/SGML authoring, it can handle either markup smoothly. That is why it has been around for so long and why it continues to be a product of choice. From simple to the most complex, Editor can handle it all.

The Arbortext suite of products

Figure 3. Arbortext Editor screen shot

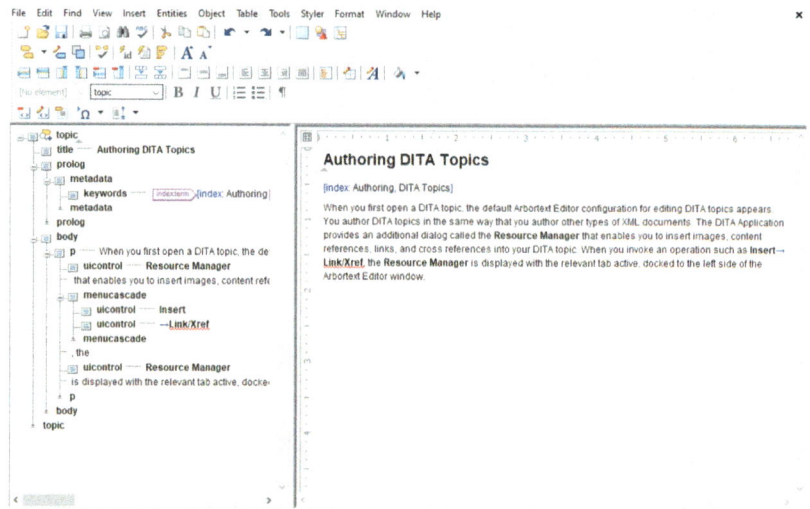

Illustrations

If you have technical illustrations in your content, then there are two solutions to choose from in the Arbortext suite. IsoDraw for isometric illustrations and Creo Illustrate for three-dimensional illustrations. IsoDraw is an easy-to-use solution that has been around for many years. You can use CAD data to create your drawings and it is great for 2D illustrations.

Figure 4. IsoDraw for technical illustrations screen shot

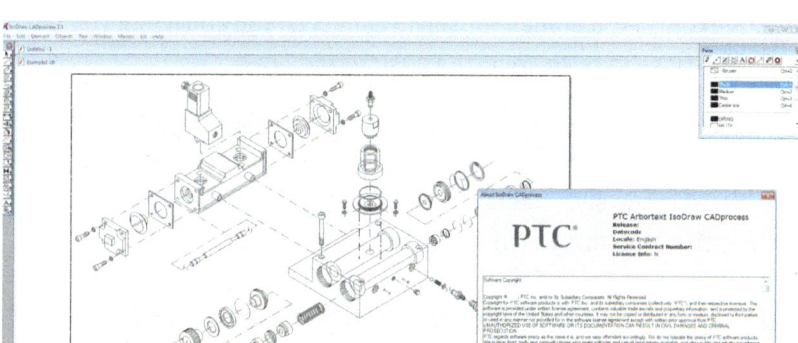

17

Creo Illustrate allows you to design rich, 3D interactive technical illustrations. If you are looking to the future and IVR or A/R (augmented reality), then this is the illustration tool to use.

Figure 5. Creo Illustrate

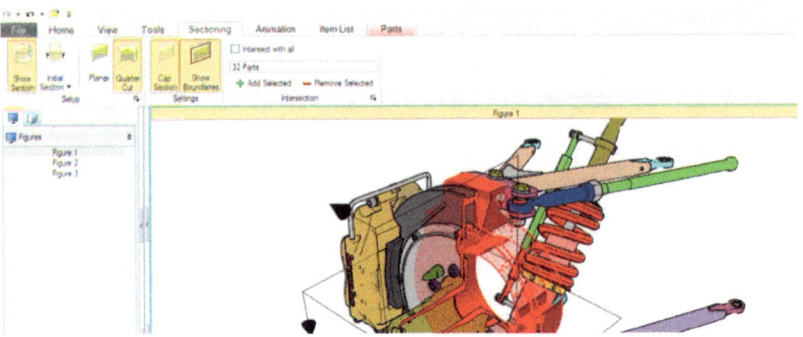

Stylized for final output

Styler is the tool we use to create style sheets that control the final output "look and feel." It instructs the publishing engine. In Arbortext, style sheets are what we use to transform authored content into output for print, PDF, HTML and Web pages, HTML Help, Rich Text, and wireless devices. There is support for foreign language including the challenges of right to left versus left to right content flow.

Arbortext Styler is a complex tool that is capable of a great many things. However, you do not need to be a programmer to use Arbortext Styler! It comes with style sheets already built that you can use as a base to build your own customized ones.

If this seems a bit daunting for you, you can always contract that work out, or better yet, hire someone who will teach you as they build it. We have built many style sheets for our customers and we always emphasize educating them along the way. After all, you will own the solution and that means you will need to be the point person for your company. So, it's better for you to be knowledgeable. What if you need to make a change? Just like tools evolve so does your content and your company needs. Imagine how much easier it would be if you knew how to build or modify your style sheet yourself. You *can do it* and I know you can because I learned how to build style sheets in Arbortext.

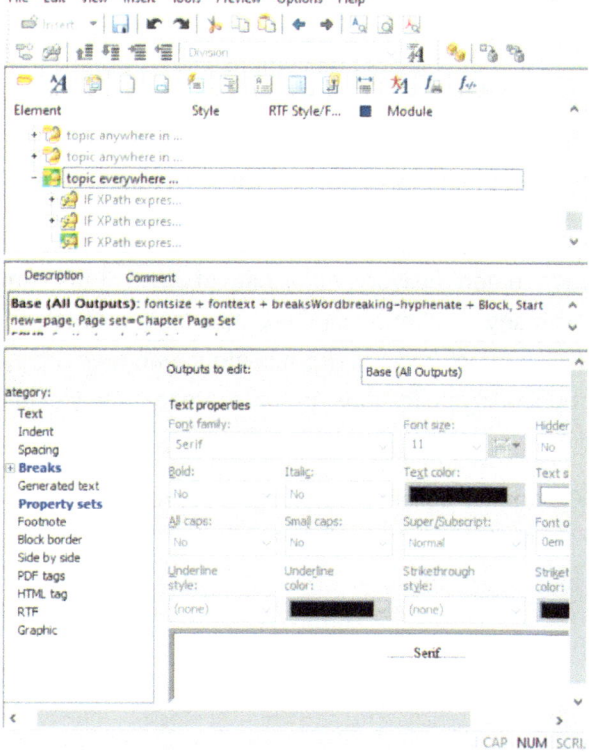

Figure 6. Styler

If you want to learn more about Styler and build your own style sheets, you can contact us or find detailed step-by-step instructions in our *Arbortext 102* book.

There is another tool that is used to direct the publishing engine called Arbortext Layout Developer. It is a very sophisticated tool that can unlock even more of the publishing capabilities. There is nothing you cannot do with Layout Developer. Due to its sophisticated nature it is a great deal more complex to master. Perhaps, one day, a book will be written for that tool. But for now, we recommend you hire one of the expert consulting teams who have mastered this tool. You can find our strategic partners—the ones we have worked with and the ones we have recommended—listed on our website.

Composition

As with the rest of the pieces that comprise the Arbortext tool suite, the composition engine has evolved to keep pace with changing demands. Arbortext Publishing Engine is the part of the suite of products that accommodates the omnichannel output.

You can achieve anything and everything you could possibly want or need for your content delivery. Publishing to any output in any language with any number of complex layouts. You can use structured or unstructured data from content management systems and other business applications. It is all there for you, you just need to command it.

The PTC Arbortext Publishing Engine is a server-based product so give it the space it needs to work its magic.

The Arbortext suite of products

Figure 7. Publish from the Editor window

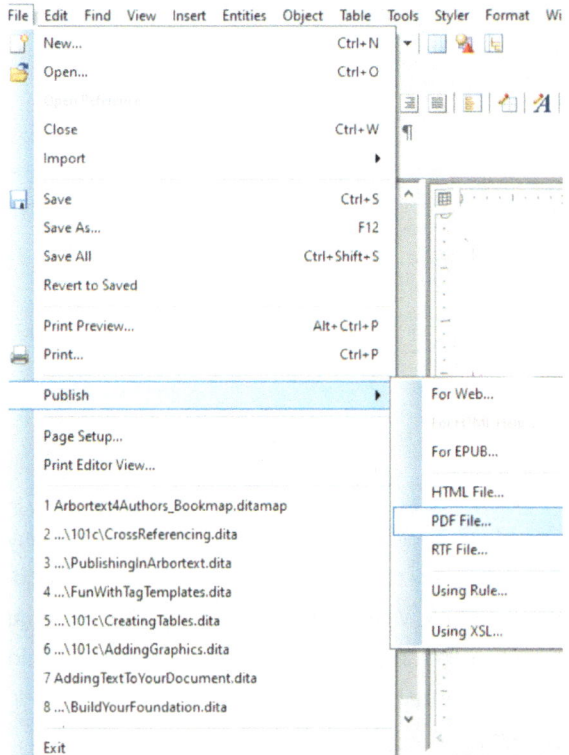

Content management and delivery

PTC's Windchill is the piece of the solution suite that manages all your content. All your information pieces and parts get stored here. From the structured XML content to the unstructured pieces, all your content can be organized and optimized for accuracy, applicability, with rich, graphics-driven delivery. Windchill allows you to work more efficiently as a team. By checking in and checking out of the workspace, you know who has what at any given moment, so you minimize the risk of redundancy or overwriting work.

If you plan on authoring in DITA—or if you work with a team larger than one—you should seriously consider a true content management

Arbortext for Authoring

solution. There are others out there to look at. We like Windchill because it works and works well with the rest of the Arbortext ecosystem.

Figure 8. Windchill's web-based interface

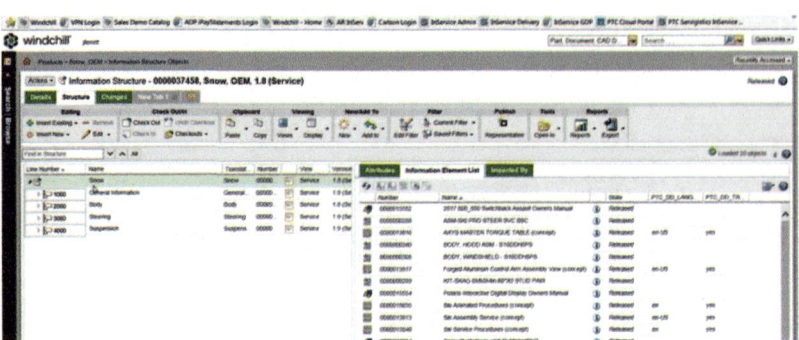

Windchill's interface is web based which makes it very easy to deploy to work teams and easy to access. You can coordinate and operate from multiple locations. With the easy visibility and rules based managed access Windchill also gives you automatic revision control on any and all the content pieces. This is a huge bonus if you are in a regulated industry.

Chapter 3. You may know more than you realize

Topics Covered in this Chapter

♦ Set up a local playground

Before we open Editor and get going, let's take a look at some of the things that you already know how to do, even if you have never opened Editor before.

Arbortext really is so easy a child could do it. In fact, if you've ever written an e-mail or used an office software program to write a letter than you will feel right at home in Arbortext Editor.

The same handy shortcuts you already use, you can use in Editor.

Table 1. Handy shortcuts we all use

Arbortext Editor	Other Software Tools
Bold	Bold
Italics	Italics
Bullets	Bullets
Editing Content	Editing Content
Inserting a Paragraph	Inserting a Paragraph
Copy, Cut, and Paste (Ctrl+C, Ctrl+X, Ctrl+V)	Copy, Cut, and Paste (Ctrl+C, Ctrl+X, Ctrl+V)
Undo (Ctrl+Z)	Undo (Ctrl+Z)
Tables	Tables

Arbortext for Authoring

Arbortext Editor	Other Software Tools
Graphics	Graphics
and the list goes on....	and the list goes on....

Arbortext Editor has some other handy features that make life much easier for authoring.

Table 2. Going beyond the basics

Arbortext Editor	Other Software Tools
You can change your editing environment to suit your personal needs without ever affecting the final output.	Nope. Can't do that because what you see is what you get so any change here may corrupt the style. The style is hard coded to the content.
Split Window with a dynamic Document Map view for navigation and for editing and/or authoring purposes.	You may have a split window but it's really for navigation purposes only.
Moving entire content chunks by moving elements around and seeing exactly where you are in the document.	I can drag content, but large chunks can pose challenges and it can be difficult to track where you are in the document.

Arbortext Editor	**Other Software Tools**
Tags On, Off, or partial. Tags allow you to see exactly what you are doing and where you are at all times.	What Tags?
Editor enforces the rules of the DTD so you cannot put things where they don't belong.	Desktop tools may not even know there are rules. You may be able to implement some templates but nothing more than that.

Set up a local playground

For this guidebook, you'll want to work with sample content before you jump into production work. It will make things much easier for you to keep all your content in a "playground" folder on your desktop. That way, once you have walked through the exercises, you can easily wipe your desktop clean and jump into production work.

What happens in the playground stays in the playground!

Who doesn't love a good junk drawer or miscellaneous cupboard? Don't get me wrong, I love a good orderly home and I like everything to have a place, but I always set aside at least one hidden area where I can clutter. Keeping my disorder contained makes it much easier for me to keep the rest of the house in order. It also makes it much easier to get rid of things that I no longer need.

That is what your playground folder is for you during this training. A virtual junk drawer where you can keep all the pieces in one place and not worry about it mixing in with your other files. You will see how the number of files can grow to a point you won't be able to keep it straight without putting it in its own container, especially if you plan on trying the DITA exercises! Stay tuned for that one and you will

Arbortext for Authoring

experience firsthand why a true component content management solution becomes paramount.

Here is what I have:

As you can see, I like a clean desktop. I have my playground folder ready for all my important pieces and a place to save my results.

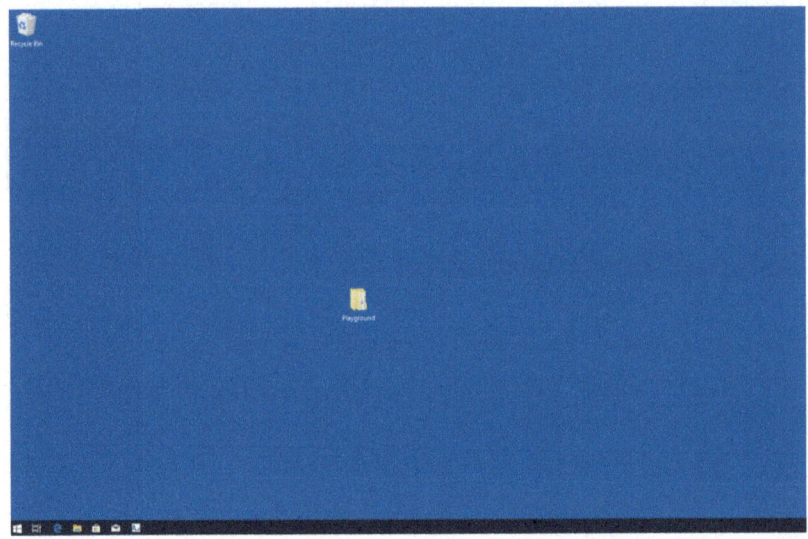

Chapter 4. Getting familiar with Arbortext Editor

Topics Covered in this Chapter
- Opening Arbortext Editor
- Opening a new sample file
- Using the split window screen
- Viewing markup
- Setting screen preferences
- Setting up your view

This book does not cover every feature in Arbortext, but it does cover enough to get you started and enough to complete one simple document start to finish. Arbortext Editor is a very robust, dependable tool that can do just about anything you could ever want an authoring tool to do.

Three things you will hear me say over and over if you are ever in my live training sessions:

- If you don't know what it is or does, click on it and find out. Because Arbortext is a robust tool with lots of wonderful features, chances are you won't break it; so, click on it. What's the worst that could happen? This is your time to experiment.

- Where your cursor is, is the key so always know where you are. *"If you don't know where you've come from, you don't know where you're going."*

    —Maya Angelou

    In Arbortext you should know where your cursor is at all times. It determines what you can do and where you are headed.

- There is almost always more than one way to do what you need to do in Arbortext. Find the method that works best for you by experimenting with all the options.

Arbortext for Authoring

Opening Arbortext Editor

Just like any other software application you click to open it. Obvious, I know, but I bring this up so you can see that the developers of Arbortext have worked hard to make sure the user experience is smooth and effortless. They continue to make enhancements and improve the user experience and Editor continues to be dependable, reliable, and predictable.

When you open Editor, you can see firsthand that it operates much like any other user-friendly software. You launch the program just like any other desktop application: click on the icon or find the application in your application list.

When you open Editor, the view looks very familiar. It has the usual drop down menus, navigation icons, and keyed shortcuts that we have all come to expect in any software we use. Roll your mouse over the icon to see what it does if it's not obvious by the picture. The creators of the software wanted to make sure you could be successful and a key piece of that is in how easy the tool is to use. Arbortext Editor feels familiar even if you have never opened it before.

Figure 9. Insert graphic using toolbar icon

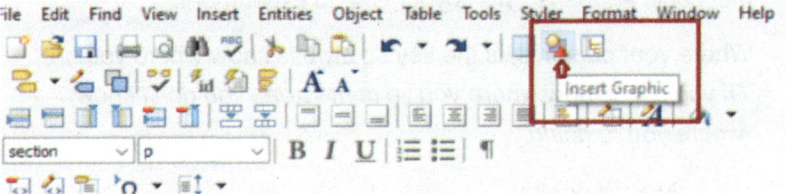

Click one of the menus in the top navigation. Notice the options that are available for you to choose versus those that are greyed out.

Opening a new sample file

Figure 10. Insert graphic using menu item

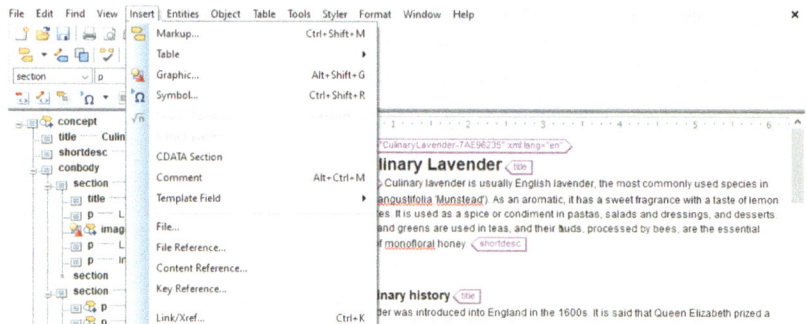

This is all behavior we have all come to expect. The look and the actions all seem familiar.

Keep Editor open for the next exercise.

Opening a new sample file

If you ever find yourself stuck or you want to try an experiment with elements, open a sample file. Sample files will have content and markup already included.

1. There is more than one way to open a new file in Arbortext. Here are some methods for opening any new file, whether it is a sample file or a template file:

    - Click on the **New File** icon on the task bar
    - Select **New** from the **File** drop-down menu
    - Enter the command key **Ctrl+N**

2. Select a Document Type from the **Category**.

Arbortext for Authoring

3. Select the **Type** of document

Figure 11. Open a new sample file

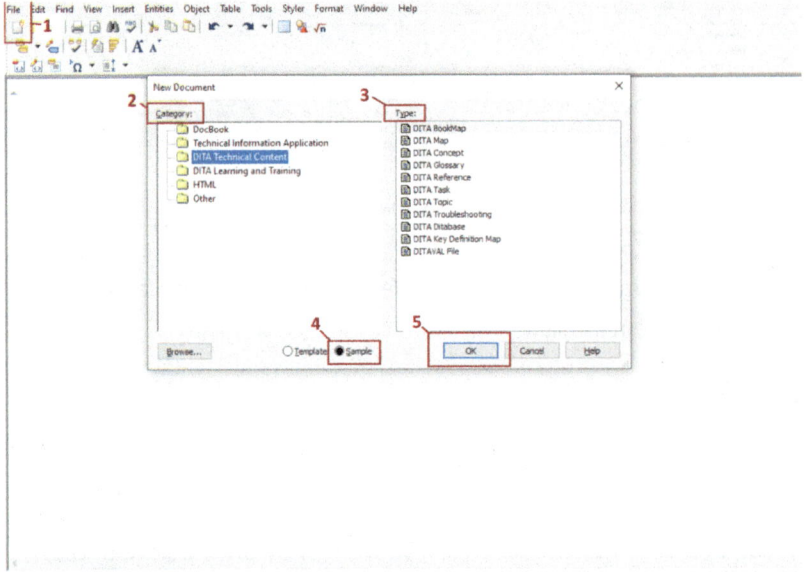

4. Select a Template or a Sample file.

   - *Template:* A template file gives you the shell with some basic markup already in place but no text or other content.

   - *Sample:* A sample file will give you a pre-populated document with text and other content pieces already embedded.

5. Select Sample and click **OK** to open the Sample file.

Keep the Sample open for the remaining exercises in this chapter.

Using the split window screen

In Arbortext Editor you can divide the screen into two unique views of the same document. The Document Map view shows you the outline view of the document and the Edit Window shows you the document in full.

Viewing markup

Having two unique views of your document at one time may feel a bit awkward at first, but it won't take long for you to discover the many advantages to having this option. For me, when I was first learning the tool, this feature felt bizarre and a little uncomfortable. But I kept it on and quickly learned the strategic value of using the Document Map. Document Map view makes it easy to drill down to specific elements and attributes, to navigate to a specific location in the document, and to move element blocks around. In fact, most of my favorite time-saving strategies are executed in the Document Map.

To make changes to the split window screen view, drop down the menu under the options on the top navigation bar.

Figure 12. Changing the window view

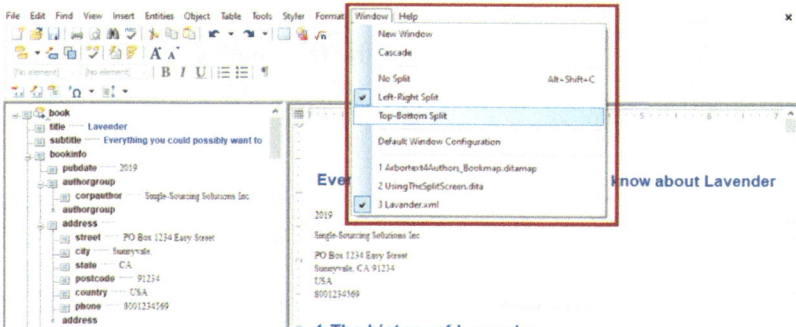

Try each of the options to see what happens to your view.

Keep this file open for the next exercise.

Viewing markup

With Editor you can choose to view what you want. You can see all the markup that defines your content, or you can turn it off. The advantage of keeping the tags on is that it will be tremendously helpful for you in keeping track of where your cursor is.

31

You do not need to be a programmer or a ninja markup master to use Arbortext Editor. There are plenty of places for you to go to look up meanings and get additional help whenever you may need. But you do need a solid sense of where you are and what you can do at all times. You need to know if you are inside or outside of an element and where that element is in relation to the next level tag. The best way to do this is with Tags on.

In the Edit Window the tags appear in a special iconic box with one tapered edge on the right or on the left depending on if it is an opening or closing tag. In the Document Map, each new element creates a new shoot off the document tree.

Click on the Tag icon to adjust the tag display. The full tag display will show you the full markup.

Figure 13. Change the tag display

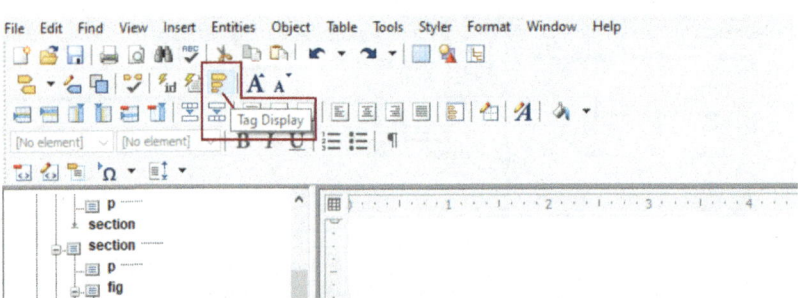

Partial tag display will show you the boundaries of the markup, where it begins and where it ends, but not the markup. You can see the opening and the closing of any element but you can't tell what the element or any attributes are until you open the markup.

Figure 14. Show partial tags

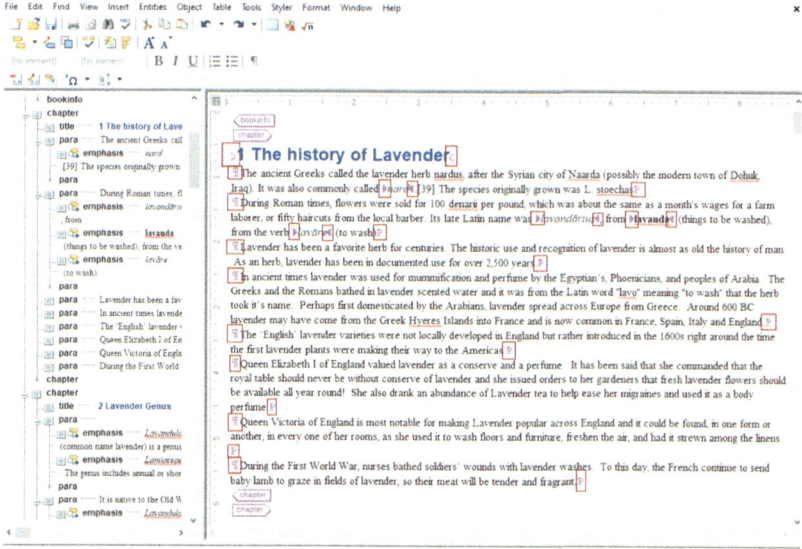

One more click and the tags will disappear completely.

You can decide how you want to work—Tags on or Tags off. Personally, I would encourage you to keep them on and in full view.

Keep this file open for the next exercise.

Setting screen preferences

Preferences allow you to modify your Editor interface view.

For example, I like my tags to show up in a hot pink color, so I change my preference. I also like to make sure the table tool bar only shows up when I'm working with tables. The key here is that you can set the preferences you want. I like to see all my options on the menu, so I always make sure I select Full Menu on the window.

1. Go to **Tools** on the top menu bar and drop down the menu.
2. Select **Preferences** from the list.

Arbortext for Authoring

3. Choose any of the categories in the left-hand pane for specific properties to change and this will open up the options.

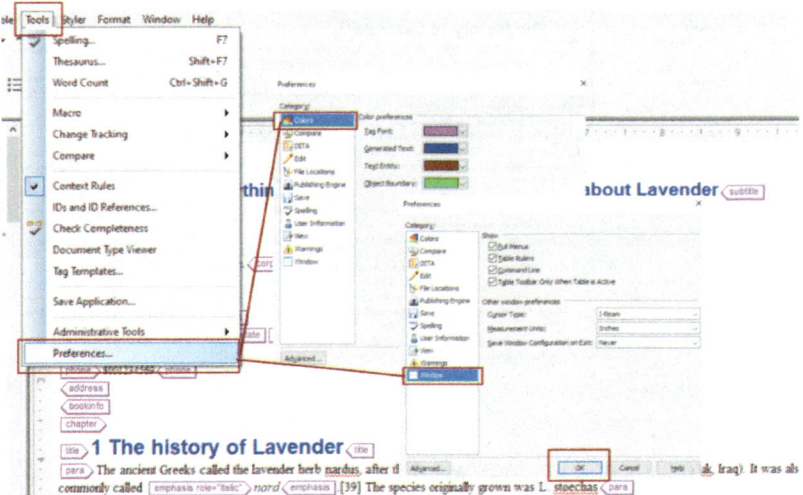

Figure 15. Setting up user preferences

4. Make the adjustments for all the categories you want to change.
5. Click the OK button to lock in your choices.

Keep this file open for the next exercise.

Setting up your view

Ever have one of those days you just need a little extra help with the font size? Well the good news is you can blow up the size of the font and not affect the output.

I know it can't be just me who has squinted at the screen and wondered if there was a period punctuation or not. Or doubted if your cursor was inside or outside of the punctuation. This is an example of one of those times blowing up the font with a simple click has been tremendously helpful for me.

Setting up your view

You can change one side or the other or both. This really comes in handy for me when I need large font in the Edit view so I can see exactly where I am but I want smaller font in the Document Map so I can see a higher level of the document.

1. Place your cursor anywhere inside the window where you want to change the font size.
2. Click on the big A icon to increase the font size and click on the small A icon to—you guessed it—decrease the font size. You can adjust the Document Map side and the Edit Window or both at the same time.

Figure 16. Increase or decrease the font size

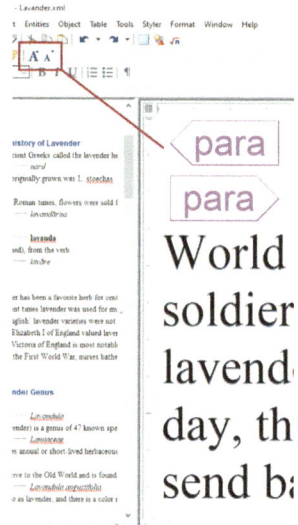

Expert tip!

Remember where your cursor is since this will dictate which side of your workspace gets the adjustment. Cursor placement is everything.

35

Arbortext for Authoring

You can now close this file. You will not need it for the next exercises so **do not save** it.

Chapter 5. Well-formed and valid documents

Topics Covered in this Chapter
- Create a well-formed document
- Create a valid document
- Change or delete markup
- Move an element
- Expand and collapse
- Inserting comments

Now that you are getting familiar with the basic authoring window it's time to roll up your sleeves and start authoring some content. We'll begin by exploring well-formed and valid documents.

Well-formed and valid content—the two are not mutually exclusive. You can have well-formed XML content but that doesn't mean it is valid. In order for a document to be well-formed the XML must follow some specific language rules. Some of the rules are:

- The XML has an opening and a closing tag. You can't have a half of a tag. If you open it, you have to close it.

- The order of opening and closing tags is strictly followed. For example, if you have a <chapter > with a <section > that is followed by a <para> , you need to close them in reverse order </para> </section> </chapter>.

- Wile you can have more than one attribute in an element, there can only be one unique attribute ID in an element.

- There can be only one root element in an XML document.

In Arbortext, the architecture or Document Type is enforced by the DTD. The DTD is in the background making sure that when you author you keep in line with the document rules. So, a document that conforms to the DTD is valid.

If the talk of well-formed and valid sounds foreign to you, don't worry. We are going to walk through a couple of exercises that should help make it very clear.

For the exercises that follow, you'll need to gather up content pieces. For now, you only need text so there is no need to gather more than what may fill a section or two in a small manual.

Here is what I have:

I like to use unrelated content like information on plants or cooking. I will be creating an imaginary book on lavender because I can find a wide variety of content pieces readily available.

Create a well-formed document

Form is the foundation of structured authoring. It has rules that the content structure must abide by regardless of the document type.

You recall how to start a new file from the exercise we did when opening a new sample file (see Opening a new sample file). We will do a very similar thing for this exercise, but we are going to create a free-form document in order to experience how to use some of the rules for well-formed documents.

1. Since we are only concerned with creating a well-formed document, select **Other** from the **Category** list.

Create a well-formed document

2. Select **Free-form** XML from the **Type** list.

Figure 17. Create new Free-form document

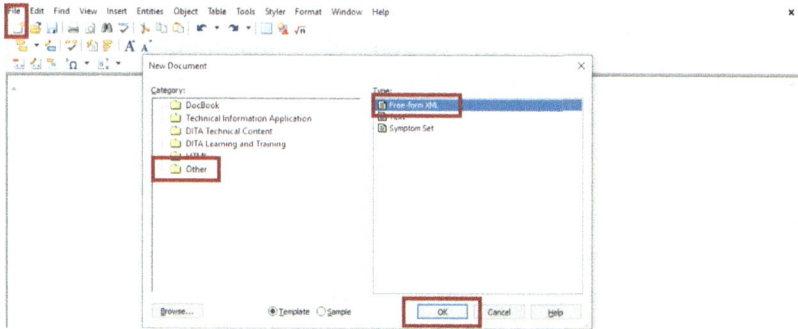

3. Click **OK**.

4. Assign the Top Level Element name. Arbortext will use Document as the default but you can change it to whatever you want. This element is only used once in the document.

   Note

   Remember well-formed rules dictate that there must be a root element which holds all the other elements. It is the container for the entire document.

Figure 18. Assign Top Level Element tag

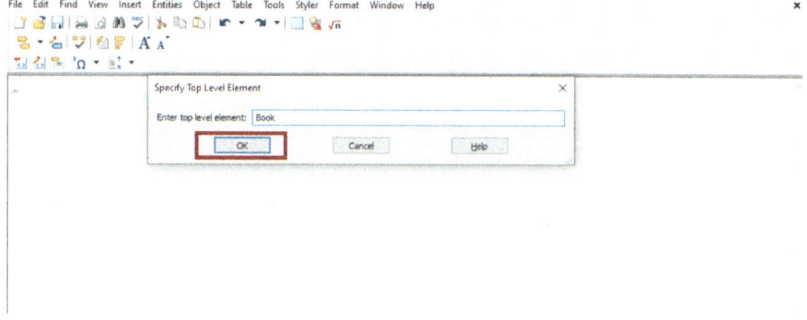

39

Arbortext for Authoring

5. Select **Markup** from the **Insert** drop-down menu. Since we are in a Free-form document, there are no elements to structure your content with.

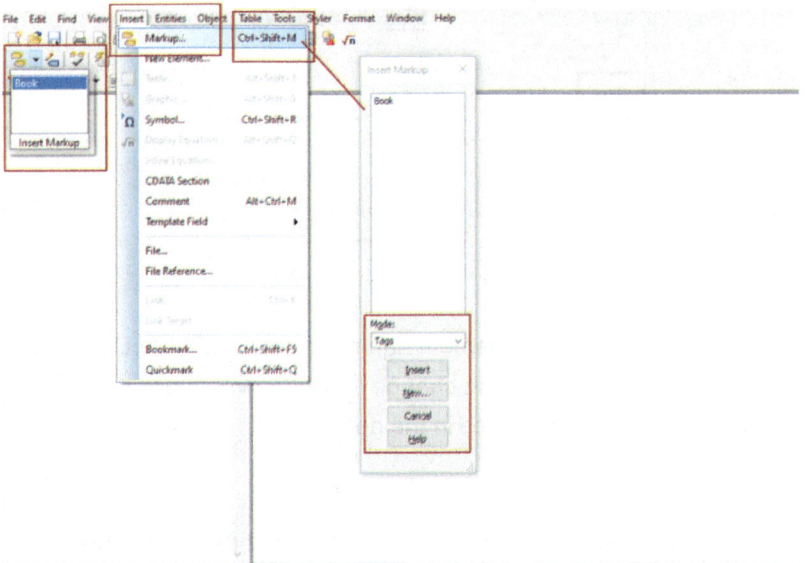

Figure 19. Ways to pull up the Markup list

Create a well-formed document

6. Create the markup for your well-formed document. Select the **New** button. Continue creating the elements that build the document like chapter, section, title, paragraph, etc.

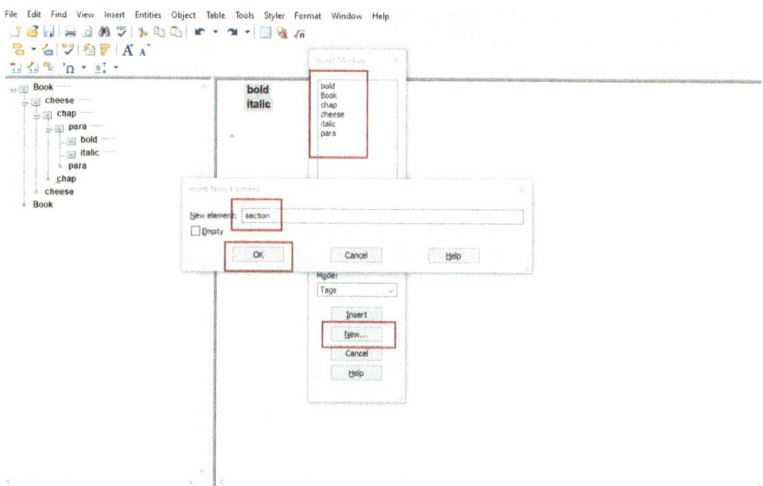

Figure 20. Make up your own markup

41

7. Add some content to your document using the Markup tags you just created. A paragraph or two is all you need, so don't make it complicated.

   Here is what I have:

   Figure 21. Sample of well-formed markup

   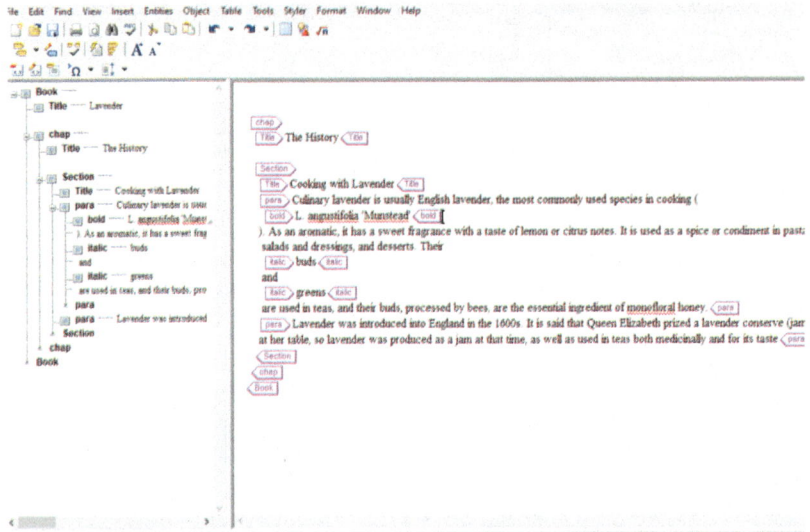

Create a well-formed document

8. To see what your final output looks like you'll need to publish. Publishing is easy. From the **File** drop-down menu select **Publish** then select **PDF File** from the sub menu.

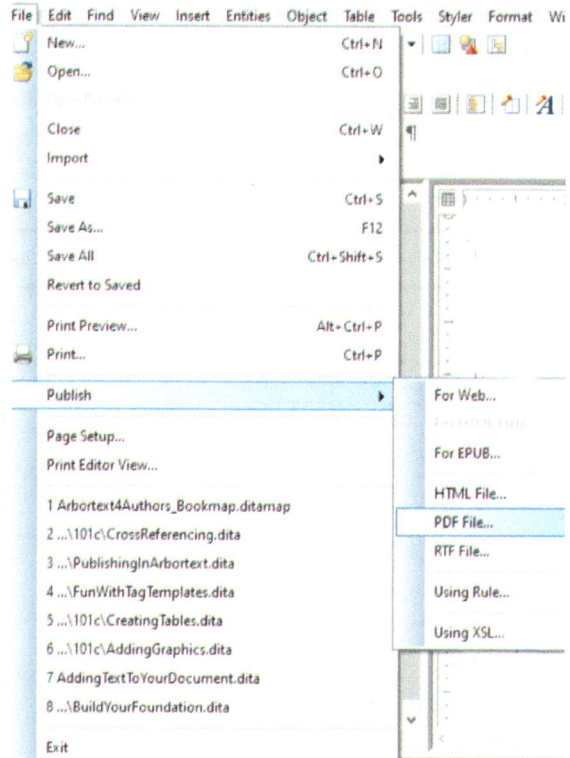

Figure 22. Finding the Publish menu item

43

9. The **Output** menu will appear. From here you can select the save document location and verify the style sheet used for composition.

   Note

   Arbortext defaults to Public Desktop. Some of you may not have access to this so make sure you select a location you can access.

   Figure 23. Publish window

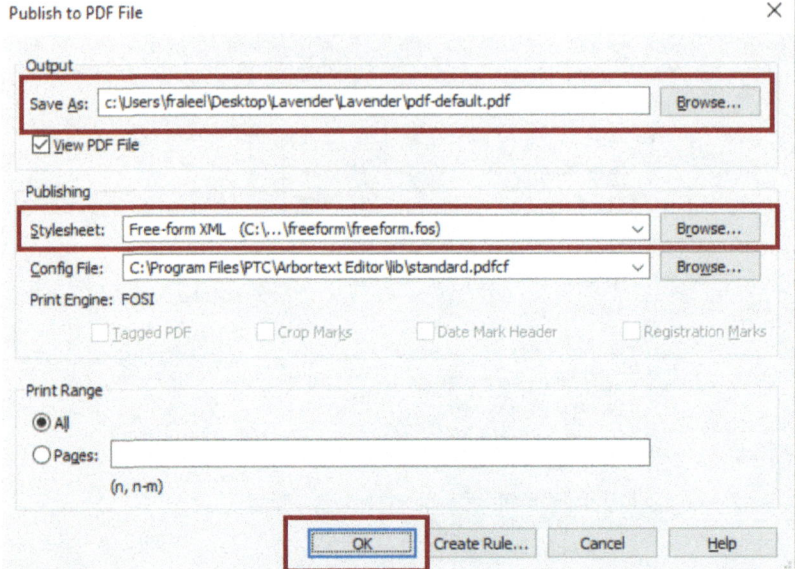

Check your results. Did you get a block of content pushed together with no style? That's what you should expect since our document was well formed but not valid to any architecture so the style sheet we used had no instructions on how to manage our made-up markup.

Here is what I have:

You can see how mine turned out in the sample images for the exercise. While I kept the markup well-formed there was no structure applied to the output. Is that what you got?

Figure 24. With no DTD, there is no formatting

Go ahead and close this file and **don't save it**. But keep Editor open for the next exercise.

Create a valid document

A valid document conforms to the rules and structure of the document types architecture.

Now that we've seen what well-formed means, let's take the next step to create a valid *and* well-formed document.

Arbortext for Authoring

1. This time you need to create a new DocBook file since we want valid well-formed content.

   Note

   Make sure you click the Template button so that we get the shell but no sample content. We will add our own content.

   Figure 25. Open a new DocBook template

   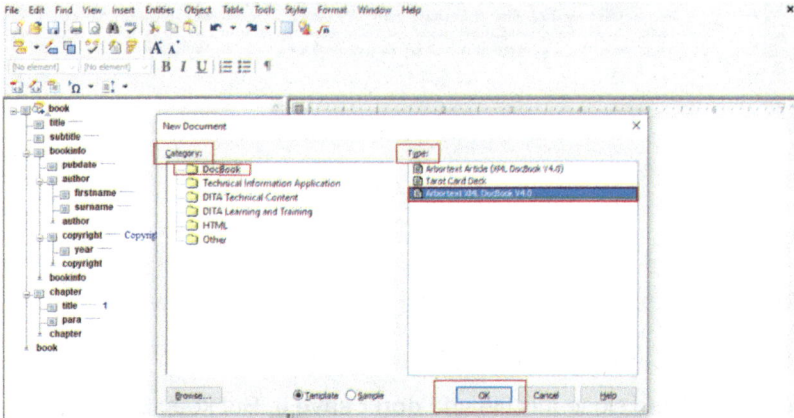

   Now when we start a new file we have a valid template to use with some basic markup already included. The DTD with the allowed Elements is loaded for us. All we need to do is add the content to the right locations with the correct descriptive markup.

Create a valid document

Figure 26. DocBook template with some basic markup

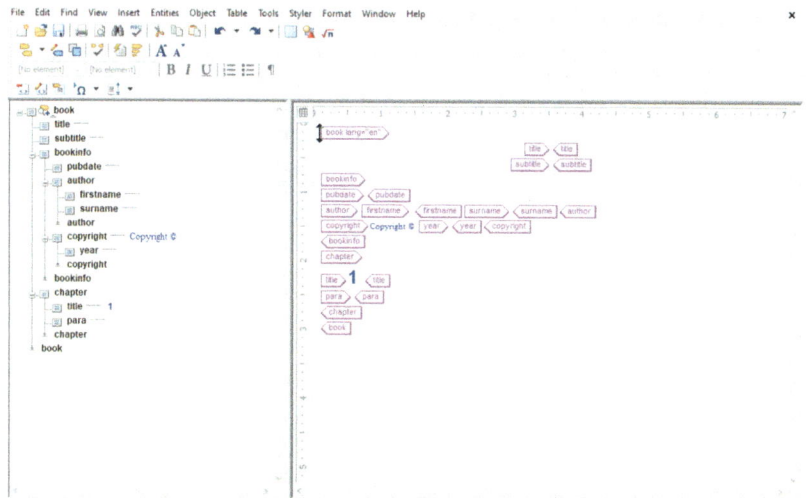

Arbortext is intelligent. You selected a DTD and Arbortext knows that typically when these documents are created there are certain markup elements that are frequently used so they are already there for you. Of course, you can add more markup and just because the markup is already there, it doesn't mean you have to use it. If you don't need it, delete it. It's better to keep your document tidy, so get rid of all open empty tags.

2. Let's start at the top. Place your cursor inside the first element set <title> </title> and type in your document title. Work your way down filling in the information as you go.

47

Arbortext for Authoring

3. Add some of the content pieces you gathered earlier. Just focus on text for now. Build enough of a content base to make it interesting—maybe a chapter with a section or two. We will add graphics and tables later so for now just focus on textual components. You can find out what type of tagging is allowed by placing your cursor where you want to add text and pulling up the list of markup.

Figure 27. Four ways to open the Insert Markup options list

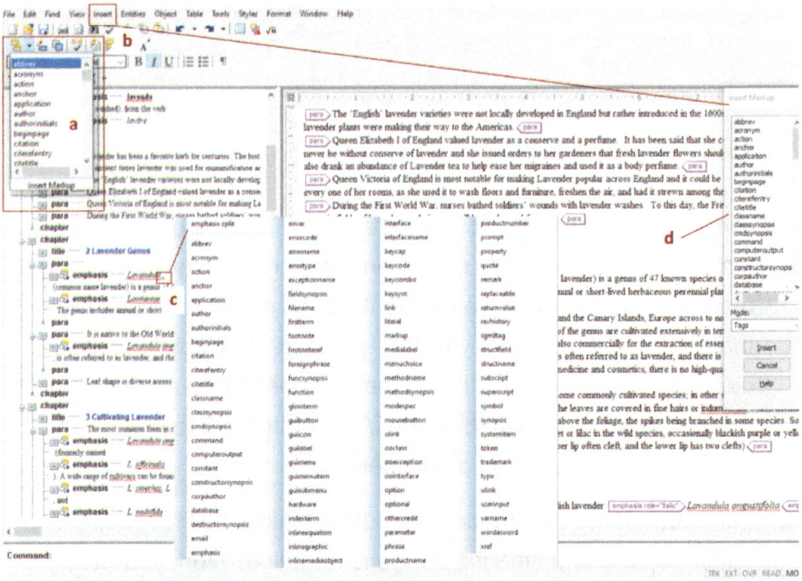

If you call up the list from the drop-down menu or the hot keys, it is easy to move it to the side, so it doesn't block your authoring windows. I find I use this method all the time for convenience.

4. Save the document and publish the PDF.

This time your composed output should look considerably different. This time you have the well-formed content but you also have a valid document that conforms to the architectural rules.

Create a valid document

5. Try going back and making some changes. Experiment with different elements and re-publish to see how they affect your output. Did the published output appear like what you had expected? Save your document. You'll use it as a foundation for the next exercise.

Expert tip!

With Arbortext, there is usually more than one way to do most anything. There are several ways to open the markup window when authoring. Try them all to find your favorite.

1. Click on the Markup icon and a list will drop down for you. Once you select the markup, the list will disappear.

2. Go to the Insert top menu. Select Markup from the drop-down menu and a list will appear in a floating window. This list will stay open as long as this document is open, even after you select your element.

3. With your cursor inside the Edit Window or the Document Map, press Enter. A list will pop up. The list will disappear once you select an element

4. For those who like to use key combinations, press **Ctrl +Shift+M** and this will bring up the list in a floating window. This list remains open even after you have selected your element.

Here is what I have:

This is much better! I know have a stylized output based on the DocBook architecture. I simply used the style sheet that came with Editor and my output has an acceptable form. Of course, if I wanted to modify the look of the output I could do that in Styler but that is a different book, *Arbortext 102*. For now, I am happy with the results.

Here is my published PDF.

Figure 28. Sample out-of-the-box Styler DocBook

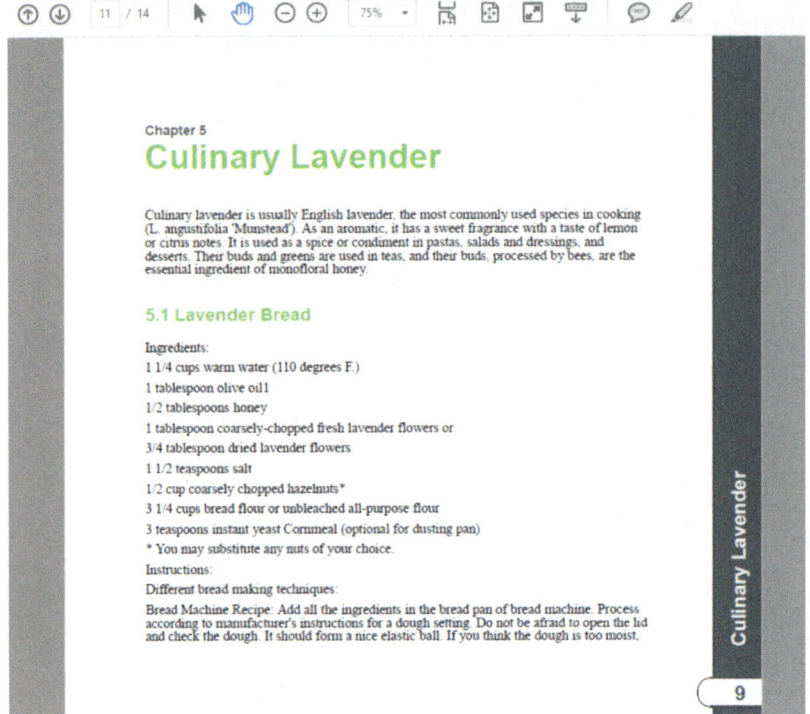

Here is my source in case you were curious.

Change or delete markup

Figure 29. Sample well-formed and valid DocBook markup

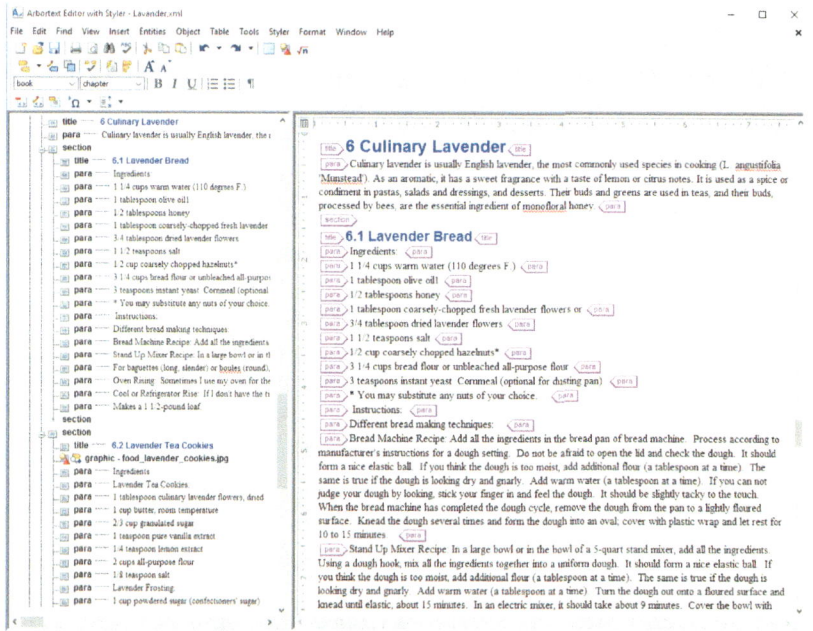

Keep this document open. You'll use it to work out the next few exercises.

Change or delete markup

While you were working on building your valid sample file, were there times you wanted to change your mind about the element to use? Did you pick the wrong tag? Not to worry; it happens to all of us. The good news is you can easily change or delete the markup in Editor.

In my list of handy things to know that can help save your sanity, I will say that the ability to change the markup easily is a great time saver.

1. Pick a word or a paragraph in your document that you want to change. Then highlight the markup from the opening to the closing tag.

51

Arbortext for Authoring

2. Select the action you want to make: Change Markup or Delete Markup

Option	Method
Change Markup	Find the icon and click on it to pull up the options to change the element. From the Edit menu, select **Change Markup**.
Delete Markup	Find the icon and click on it to pull up the options to change the element. From the Edit menu select **Delete Markup**. For those who like to use key combinations, press **Ctrl+Shift +X**

3. Experiment with markup changes that you are unfamiliar with.

   Expert tip!

   Notice you cannot change the markup to anything other than what is allowed for the location you are in. Arbortext Editor will not allow you to add elements where they are not allowed.

Here is what I have:

I selected in-line text to change from **paragraph** to **remark**.

Move an element

Figure 30. Change Markup

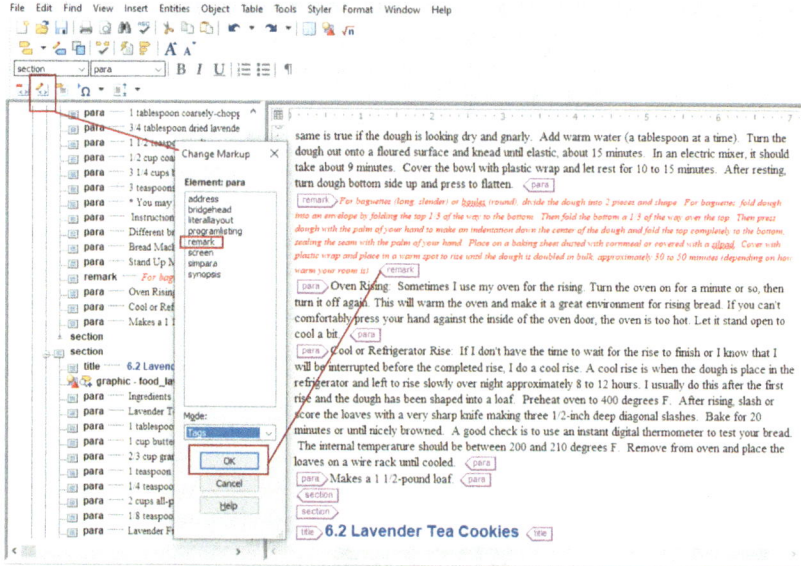

Keep your document open. You'll use it to work out the next few exercises. Save your document if you made any changes that you want to keep.

Move an element

You can move content around by highlighting the element you want to move and dragging it to the new location. You can move a small amount or a large block. It's like rearranging the living room furniture set.

There has been more than one occasion where I wrote content and in review realized that the paragraphs needed to be shuffled around. I have reorganized sections in a chapter and rearranged chapters to reorganize an entire book.

With Arbortext Editor you can do this with ease and without worry because you won't break the document since you cannot put the

Arbortext for Authoring

elements where they are not allowed. You can drag and drop elements to move them around in your document without having to copy and paste or reconstruct it. When you move an element, you move it, and everything contained in it.

I have found the ability to easily move elements around to be indispensable!

1. Highlight the element block you wish to move.

Figure 31. Move selected content to a new location

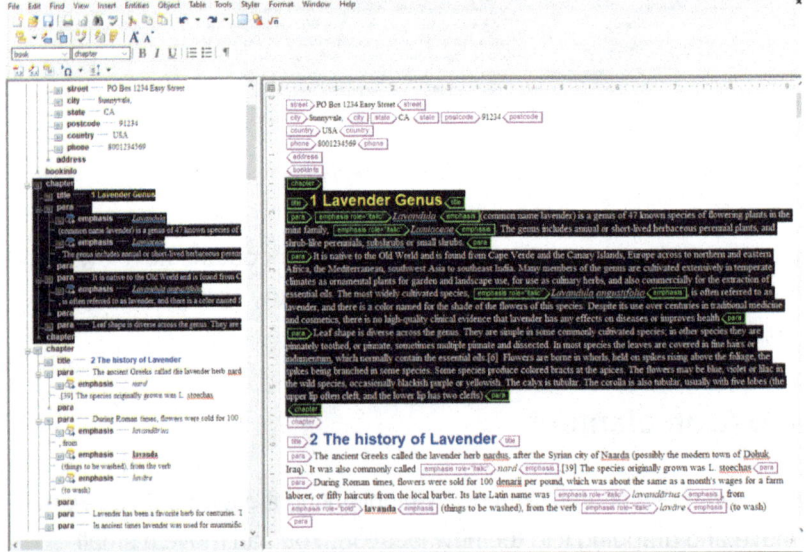

Expert tip!

I have found it much easier to use the Document Map side of the application window. It's easy to see where you are going in the tree structure of the document.

2. Move the element block to the new location.

    - In the Document Map view, hover your mouse over the tree until you see a four direction cross symbol appear. Then click and drag without releasing until you move the block to its new location.

    - From the Edit Window, hover your mouse anywhere over the highlighted block, click on it with your mouse and drag without letting go until you have reached the area you wanted to relocate the content to.

Expert tip!

It may take a bit of practice to get the hang of this one but you will eventually really come to appreciate this handy trick. You can't drop it where it doesn't conform to the valid structure, but you can drop it in the wrong place. Just remember the universal undo: **Ctrl+Z**

Here is what I have:

I rearranged the order of the chapters so that the history is now the first one.

Figure 32. New chapter order

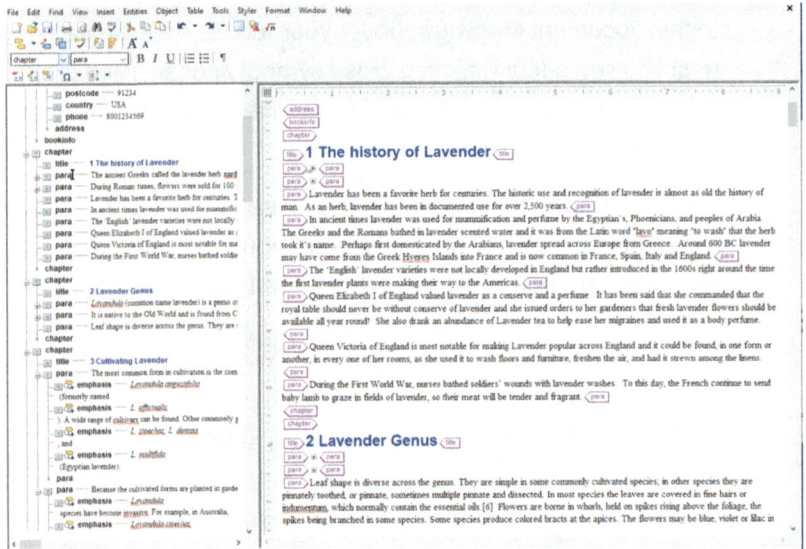

Save your work and keep this document open. You'll use it to work out the next exercise.

Expand and collapse

Ever find yourself working in large files with many sections and lots of content? How about large tables? Ever feel like your graphics are getting in your way? When content starts to get large, it becomes more challenging to navigate.

Maybe it's just me but I like to close cupboards when I am done with them. I also have a habit of closing the drawers on the dresser and shutting the closet door. You get the idea. I don't like the distractions clutter brings and when a document starts to get larger, to me it feels cluttered.

Sure, if you have made the switch over to DITA, then most of that is taken care of by the topic architecture but you still have tables to

Expand and collapse

contend with. And what about those times you may need to work in other architectures?

Learning how to expand and collapse can really help you navigate and stay sane no matter how complicated your document may become. Besides, it's a single step process. It doesn't get easier than that!

1. In the Document Map side you can see the tree structure. In case you had not noticed, the joining points often have a box with a – or a +. Sometimes, like with images and inside a table group, you can find a simple +.

Figure 33. Collapse areas of the document

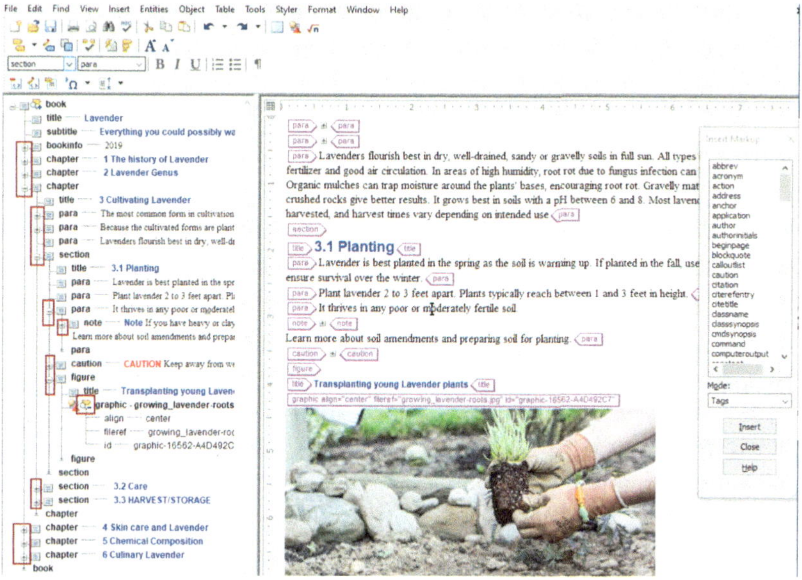

2. Click on + and watch what happens.

   By collapsing the areas I am not working in, I can see the entire book structure and where I am currently working in the document.

   Collapsing areas not being edited makes it easy to focus on what you are currently authoring. I find I use the expand and collapse option frequently and it's another reason I feel the Document Map is such a game changer when authoring.

   ### Expert tip!

   Here's a bonus tip for you. When you are working with images in your document, you don't really need to see them or have them eating up screen space. You can hide them from view by un-selecting **Graphics** from the **View** drop-down menu. To turn them back on, simply check the box next to the word **Graphics**.

Here is what I have:

The graphics were distracting and not relevant to what I was working on. I collapsed all the surrounding areas and I just needed to remove the graphic images from my view. It is easier for me to focus on what I need to do without the clutter and I know exactly where I am at in the Document Map.

You can see the element and the attributes for the graphic, just not the image for now.

Inserting comments

Figure 34. Hiding graphics from view

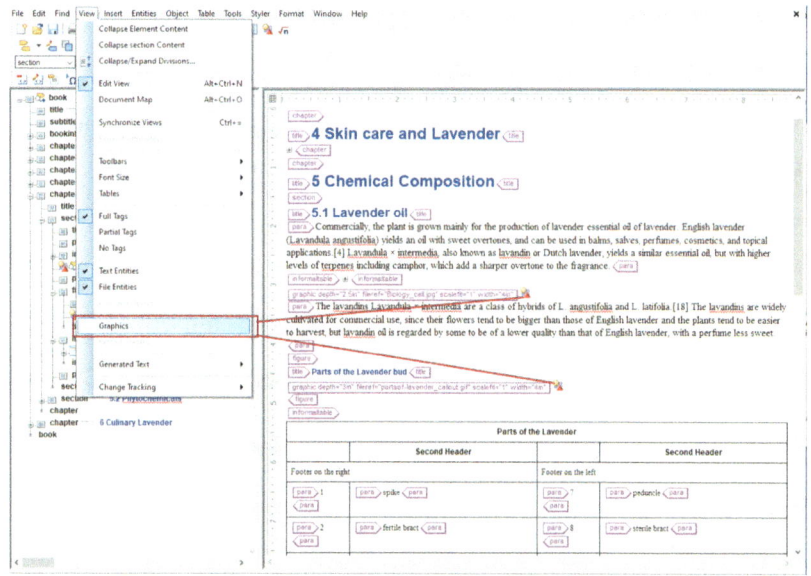

Keep this document open. You'll use it to work out the next exercise.

Inserting comments

I am sure I am not alone in this; I do something and I know why I did it at the time. But ask me weeks or months later, and I cannot remember why.

Comments are like a virtual ™Post-it note for content authors! Years ago, when I was an aspiring student of programming, one of the disciplines that was drilled into me was the importance of commenting. Fast forward to years later and I land in Tech Comm and guess what? Commenting your source files is tremendously beneficial.

- Comments allow you to keep notes with the document.
- Comments are not printed so they can only be seen in the source file.

59

Arbortext for Authoring

- Comments allow you to communicate with collaborative teams.
- You can use a comment as a reminder or a temporary placeholder.

You may see other benefits, but these alone should demonstrate the advantage of proper commenting your documents.

1. Add comments to your document. There are two ways to evoke this element.

    - From the **Insert** drop-down menu, select **Comment**.
    - For those who like to use key combinations, press **Alt+Ctrl+M**.

Figure 35. Insert comments

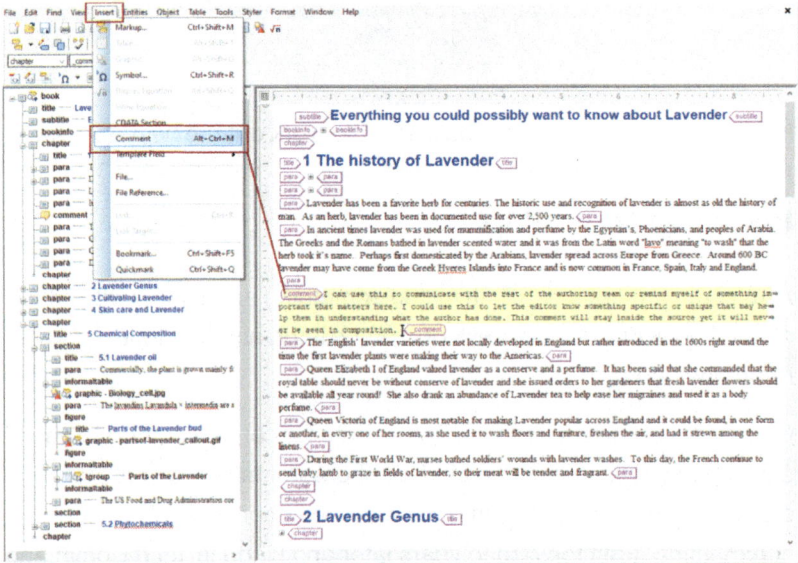

Go ahead and close this document. You could save it if you think you may want to reference it later. Otherwise close it and delete it from your Playground folder. From this point on, we will begin creating your first document.

Chapter 6. Authoring your first document

Topics Covered in this Chapter
- Build your foundation
- Adding text to your document
- Adding graphics
- Creating Tables
- Fun with Tag Templates
- Publishing in Arbortext
- Cross-referencing

Not all document types are the same. They each have their own set of rules and their specific markup. It's important to understand the specifics of the document type you are working with before you start. The architectural requirements play a key role in the decisions made when planning out your content.

Plan it out

Planning things out beforehand can help increase your efficiency and will keep you organized. It gives you the opportunity to find all your corner cases, those situations that may be complicated to solve. Knowing your content and those situations with the design architecture and associated rules, gives you the foundation of your authoring plan.

Most of our work is in this phase of the authoring process; planning and research. The more quality effort exerted here, the smoother our content creation will be. Make sure you have a solid grasp of the specifications for the architecture, any authoring rules or style guides your company may have.

Expert tip!

If you do not have style guides and authoring guides for your company, create them now. Even if you are a team of one, create these guides for your sanity and for your company. What if you won the lottery and went on a permanent vacation? How will the company know what and why you authored the way you did? What if your team grew or you had to bring in a consultant to help for a period of time? They cannot read your mind with any accuracy and you would not want them to have to intuit what to do. So, write a guide if you don't have one.

Before we start to build our document, gather the content: text, images, and tabular information plus whatever else would represent what you encounter in a normal day. In addition to textual paragraphs be sure to include step processes, itemized lists, admonitions (warnings, cautions, and notes), images, drawings with callouts, etc.

As we walk through the exercise, I will take you step by step to creating your first simple document. With Arbortext there is usually more than one way to achieve any objective. I'll highlight some options along the way. Try different techniques to find the combination that works the best for you.

What are the corner cases you see in your work? Do you have any tricky content? What is your most difficult challenge? Keep these in mind as we move forward.

Here is what I have:

My imaginary project is to author an all-purpose book about lavender. For my book I want to make sure I cover the history of the plant, the cultivation, and practical applications from topical to medicinal to culinary. I also want to include some recipes and some science.

Authoring your first document

I have gathered the content pieces that I will need, and I have a high-level idea of the main points that my book needs to cover. My content pieces reflect what I will need to create my book.

This is a good start. I may add more to it as I go, but for now it is enough.

Figure 36. Gathering the pieces for authoring

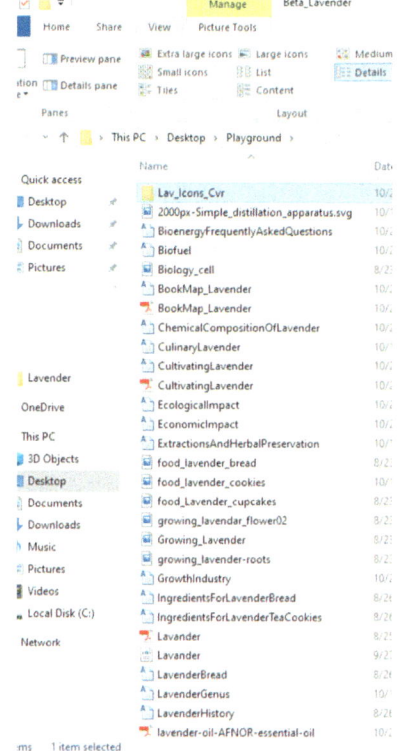

At this point, I am aware of one tricky piece for my book. I know I will have at least one graphic with call outs and a legend table. The scope of the lavender project is diverse, so I hope to have enough variety in the content I gathered to make sure I have tables and figures as well as graphics and lists.

Arbortext for Authoring

While I have no immediate need to translate, I would like to make sure I use authoring best practices for the future as well as the current needs. So, I will be considering how my markup may affect my ability to migrate later. For example, if I author in DocBook today, how would that impact moving to DITA or any other architecture in the future? What about the content consumers and their demands? Content needs to be mobile and available in small concise pieces that have a high degree of relevance to the requester. How will my authoring decisions today affect the future output?

Build your foundation

Following the rules of the document type, we will create the shell for your project so that all you need to do is insert the content that you developed in your planning.

The architecture you are building in dictates the shell structure you will create. In DocBook we have the concept of linear documents from the top down. A book has chapters with sections and subsections. DITA can have chapters as well but the organization is a collection of topics that can each stand alone. This knowledge affects how you build your shell structure.

Build your foundation

1. Open a new DocBook file, give it a title, then save it.

   Note

   It does not matter what architecture you will be authoring in—DocBook, DITA, MIL-STD, custom, or what ever the future holds—you will do this each and every time you want to create a new file or topic.

   Figure 37. Opening a new DocBook file

   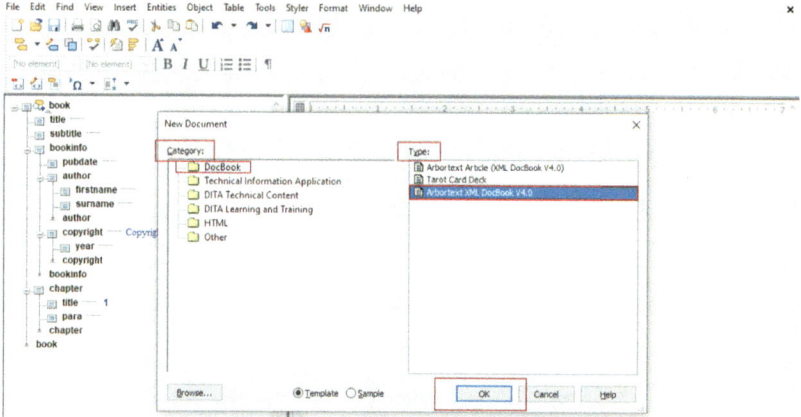

65

Arbortext for Authoring

2. Create the basic tagging structure so that all you need to do is insert the content that you developed in your planning.

   We are working with the DocBook architecture. Add your empty chapters and add your sections. Since you planned out your document, this should be a straightforward step to do.

   Figure 38. Start to build an empty shell

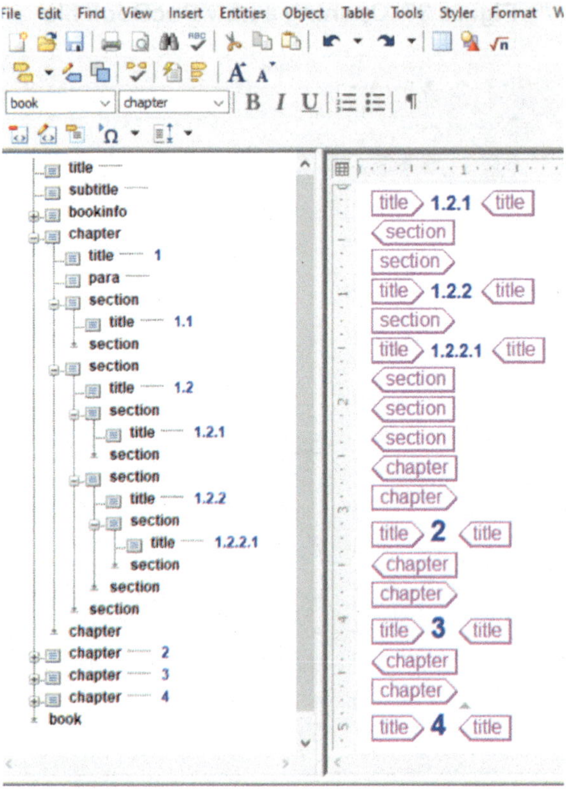

Here is what I have:

Since I am authoring in DocBook, I know the customary structure is chapters with sections and subsections. My basic layout includes chapters with working titles and sections. I've even named a few of my sections. I can always change the titles later. I know that each of my chapters will have sections so I will add a few now and change them later as needed. I will save the details for when I am ready to author. The purpose here is to have a rough sketch of a plan laid out; I know I can always move things around easy enough.

Figure 39. The beginning of my book on lavender

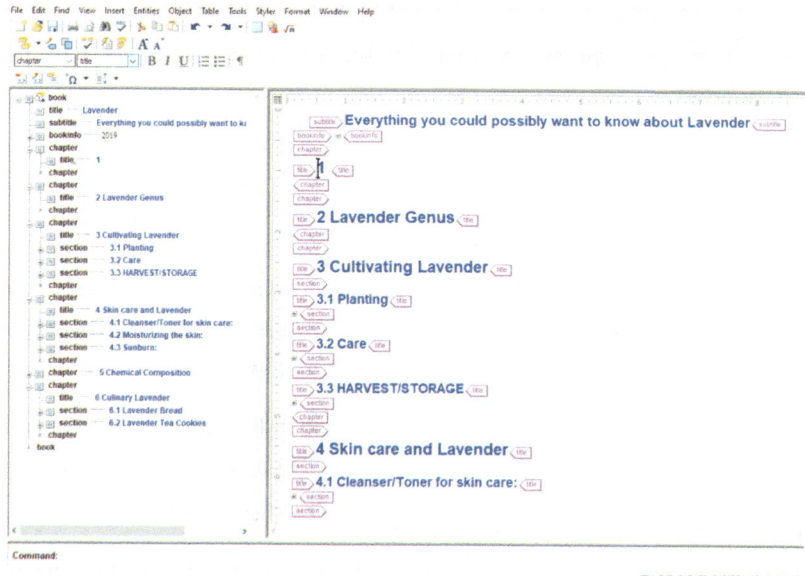

Save your work and keep this document open. You'll use it to work out the next exercise.

Adding text to your document

Time to start authoring content in your new document.

This is where all that research and planning really pays off. By the time you sit down to author the document, you will have everything you need. The most challenging—and interesting—part of writing is in the content, not the tool. The tools should just work for you. They are the canvas for your creation.

1. Place your cursor where you want to add text.

   You will recall from our past exercises that Arbortext Editor will only allow you to use acceptable markup for the location. You can view a list of allowable markup by using any one of the methods we already covered when we were building a valid document.

2. Open the Markup list and select the appropriate tag.
3. Either type in the text or paste the text in and add attributes where needed.

Repeat these steps as needed.

Here is what I have:

I have started adding more depth to my document and I have made some changes from my original draft. As I was authoring the content I re-organized some of the text to improve the flow.

When you authored your content and added in-line elements, did you notice the changes in the Document Map? The Edit Window shows the in-line of the paragraph while the tree shows the branch when a new element is introduced. This makes element search and edit much easier.

Adding graphics

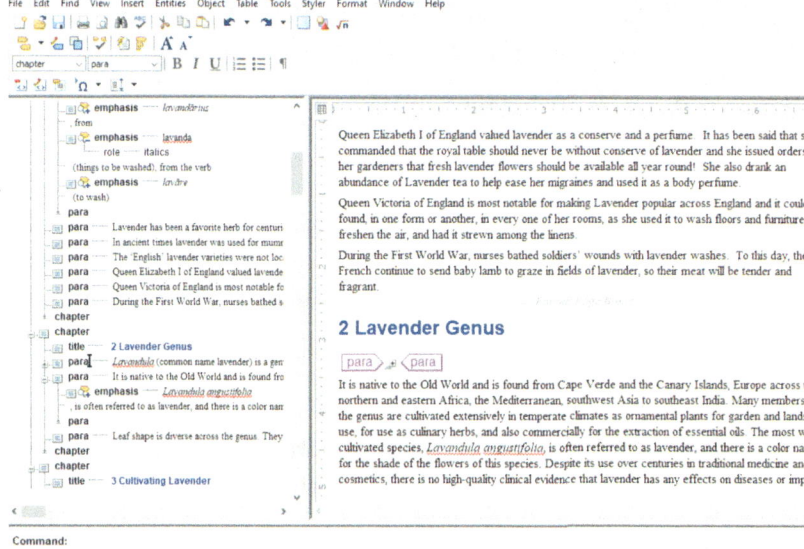

Expert tip!

You can modify the attribute in the Document Map. It's just another way you can get to what you need to do in Editor. I changed the emphasis from italics to bold.

Save your work and keep this document open. You'll use it to work out the next exercise.

Adding graphics

Adding graphics and figures to your document is very straightforward. Since Arbortext is an authoring tool, not an art tool, it makes graphics very easy to manage. Beyond inserting the graphics in the appropriate location there isn't much else to do with them.

Figures are numbered, have titles, and show up in a list of figures. They also allow for other formatting elements inside the <figure>, such as <informaltable>, to create a legend table for your image. The <graphic> does not.

69

Arbortext for Authoring

There should be very little you would ever need to do with a graphic inside an authoring tool. But there are some attributes you can manipulate. Ideally your graphics will be sized correctly before you bring them into your document, but you can enforce some sizing in Editor.

Expert tip!

For best results make sure images are at least 300 dpi.

1. Find a location in your document where images are allowed and insert an image.
2. Open the Attributes for the graphic you wish to modify. There are a couple of ways to open the Modify Attributes for any tag set.

    - One way is to place the cursor inside the tag set and then right-click on the mouse to pull it up.

    - Another method is to highlight the tag set and select the Modify Attributes icon.

Adding graphics

3. Adjust depth for the height and width for, you guessed it, width. You'll need to specify the measurement type and use the same for both sides. You cannot specify inches for one side and centimeters for the other. Just be consistent.

Figure 40. Modify the graphic attributes

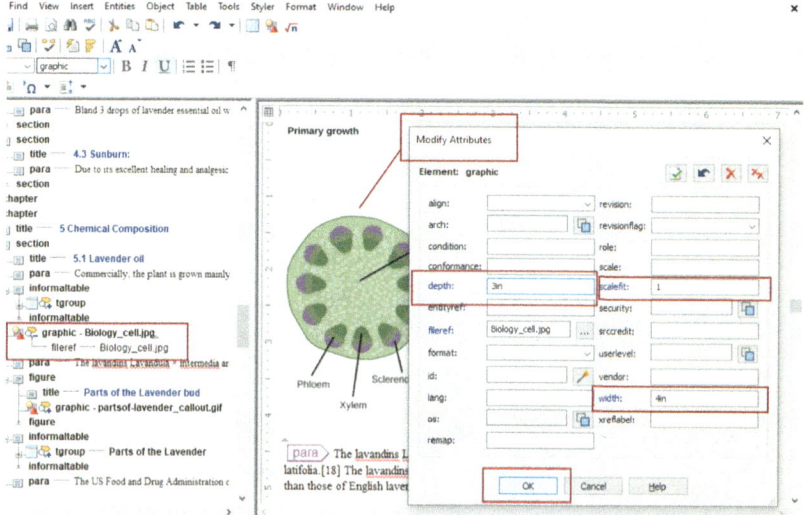

You can also see how I expanded the attributes in the Document Map view by clicking on the **+** sign. I've expanded the Document Map view so you can see the attributes assigned to this element. Personally, I feel it is easier to see the attributes in the Document Map.

Note

You should have your allowable graphic sizes listed in your authoring guide so that there is no guessing at what the correct size should be. If you don't have an authoring guide, then we need to talk!

4. Set the scalefit to 1 for the changes to take effect.

71

Arbortext for Authoring

5. Once you have finished entering information in the fields select OK for the changes to take hold.

Here is what I have:

You can see the sizing attributes in the graphic elements. What you see on the screen won't necessarily match what will be published.

Figure 41. Graphic size is modified

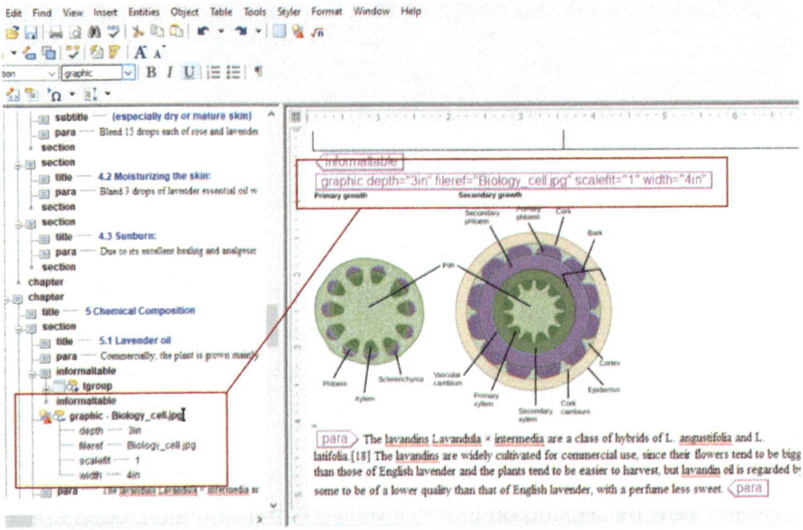

Once I finish adding all my graphics, I hide them from view so I can focus on the rest of my document.

Expert tip!

When I work in a document with a lot of graphics, the document can feel overwhelming. The graphics become big blocks that get in my way and are distracting so I like to hide them from view. The image links are still present, I just don't need to see the image. To do this, simply go to the **View** drop-down menu and un-check the **Graphics.** Reverse your steps to turn them back on view mode.

Figure 42. Hiding graphics will give you a cleaner workspace

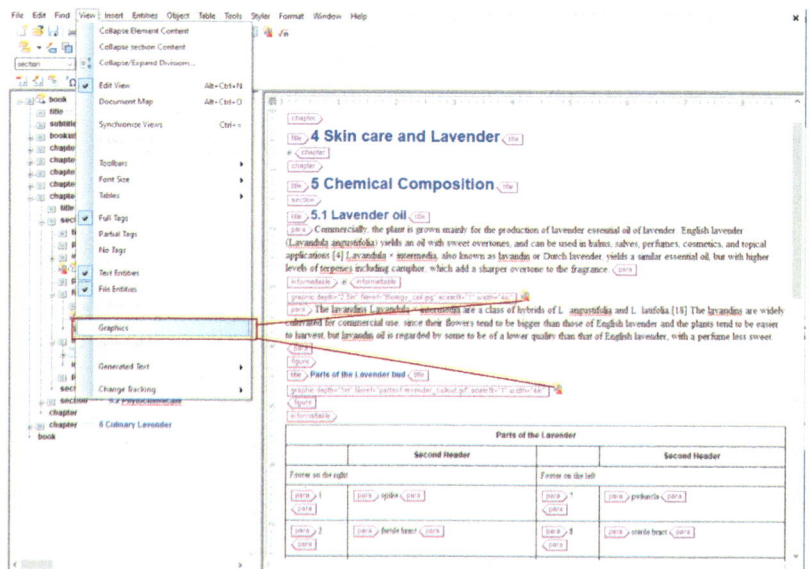

Save your work and keep this document open. You'll use it to work out the next exercise.

Creating Tables

Tables are for tabular content and not a design tool to force a layout. Authoring tables in Arbortext Editor is a breeze.

With Arbortext, the style sheet handles the final look and feel of the composed output. Beyond using the proper markup, the author has very little impact on this from the Edit Window. The one exception to this rule is with tables. What you do here can carry over to the published output. You can unintentionally override the style sheet so be very mindful in your handling of tables.

CAUTION

Be aware that what you do to tables in Editor may impact the published output.

Arbortext for Authoring

You can have a table with titles or an informal table. Titled tables will be assigned numbers and they will show in a List of Tables. Informal tables will not. And you may recall from past exercises that you can easily change the table type using the **Change Markup**.

1. Find a place in your document that allows for tables and insert a table.

   - The <table> element will give you the table with a title and will be added to the LOT (List of Tables).

   - The <informaltable> element gives you a table group with no title and thus will not show up in the LOT.

Figure 43. You can use Table or Informaltable. Switching is easy.

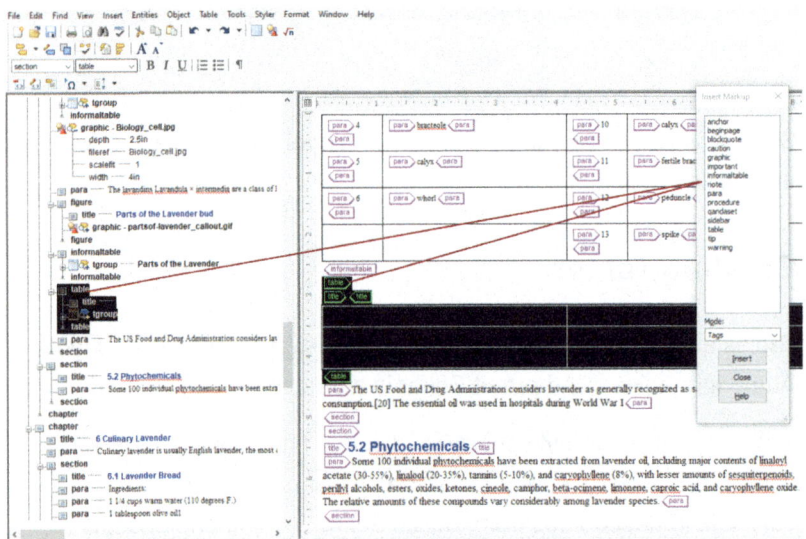

Creating Tables

2. Assign a header row and a footer row for your table.

   As we've seen, with Arbortext you can usually find more than one way to do just about anything.

   - With your cursor placed inside your table, right-click your mouse to pull up the Table menu.

   - If you set your preferences correctly then you will see that the Table markup icon is active in the top navigation.

   - You could also use the Table drop-down menu from the top navigation bar.

   - For those who like to use key combinations, there are several key combinations for tables as well.

Figure 44. Table tools

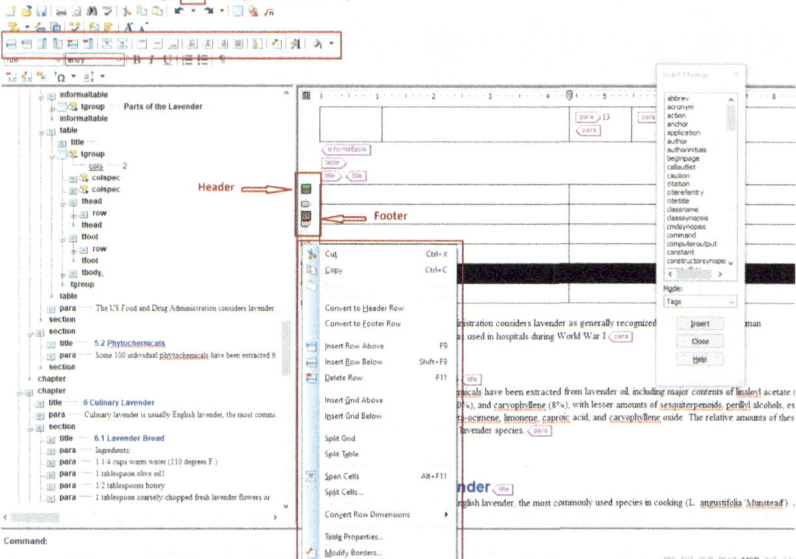

Note

You will notice the header and footer will both still show on the top of the table in the Edit Window. When you

75

compose for publication, they will be displayed in the appropriate location. To help you distinguish between the two, in the Edit Window the header row has a green bar at the side margin and the footer row has a red bar.

- Header rows will repeat at the top if your table splits over multiple pages.
- You can have more than one header row.
- Footer rows do not exist in DITA.

3. Take some time to use all the options in building your table: span cells, add rows, add columns, etc. Think about the tables you typically use and try to set up a table to reflect that.

Creating Tables

4. Set the column width by pulling up the attributes window and adjusting the <colwidth> for each column.

- Highlight the column in the Edit Window to open the Modify Table Attributes window.

- Expand the <table> in the Document Map, expand the <tgroup> and hover your cursor over the <colspec> you want to modify, right-click the mouse and the Modify Table Attributes window will pop up.

    CAUTION

    Everyone does it when they first start using Arbortext —they drag the line to try and adjust the table column width. This is a case of "Just because you can do something it doesn't mean you should do it". The proper way to adjust the column width is in the Attributes for the Table or in the Document Map. Otherwise you may end up with unpredictable results at the publishing stage.

77

Figure 45. Table width attribute

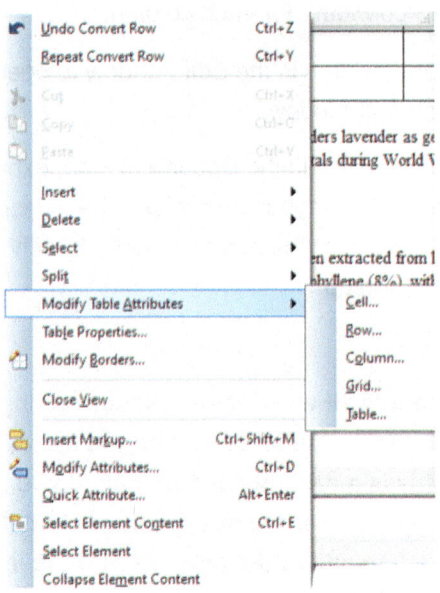

5. Set the width to the desired percentage.

   Expert tip!

   The star * represents percentage in XML table attributes. When you set one column you should set all the column widths.

Here is what I have:

I wanted to show you that I could use the Document Map side as well as the Modify Table Attributes to make my adjustments. Another example of how you can work the way you feel more comfortable with. It's good to have options.

Fun with Tag Templates

Figure 46. Modify Attributes from the Document Map or the Edit Window

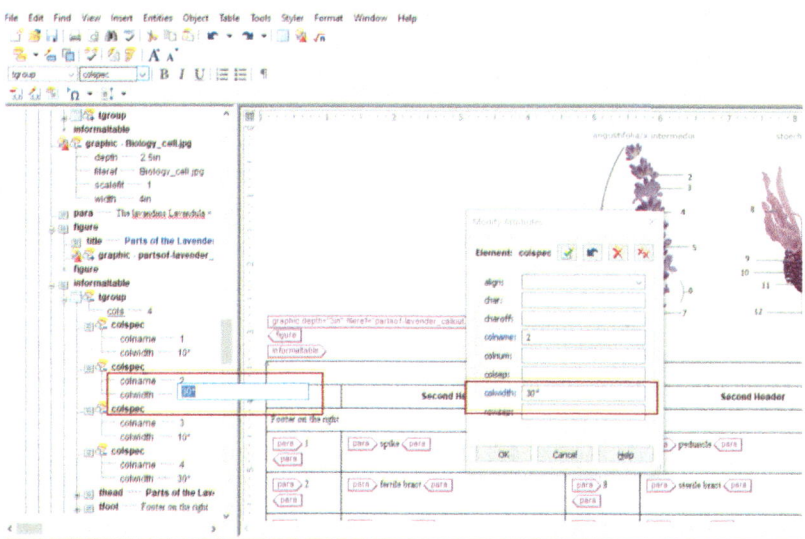

Before we leave this graphic I wanted to point out two things. This is one of my corner cases I mentioned earlier in the planning stage. I have a graphic with callouts and I need a legend table to go with it. My solution was an informal table and all columns combined equal 80% of the table width. We'll see how it looks in when we publish later.

Save your work and keep this document open. You'll use it to work out the next exercise.

Fun with Tag Templates

If you find yourself doing the same thing over and over again, then you might want to take advantage of Tag Templates. Tag Templates can insert content such as sets of instructions or a partially filled-in list that you want to use repeatedly.

Think of things you often have to repeat as you author, such as the same type of table that repeats many times.

Arbortext for Authoring

Some ideas:

- Tables
- Graphics
- Lists

For this exercise we are going to create a Tag Template for a table.

1. Find a place where tables are allowed and build a table formatted to your specifications.
2. Select the table from beginning to end.
3. Open the **Tools** drop-down menu

Figure 47. Opening Tag Templates

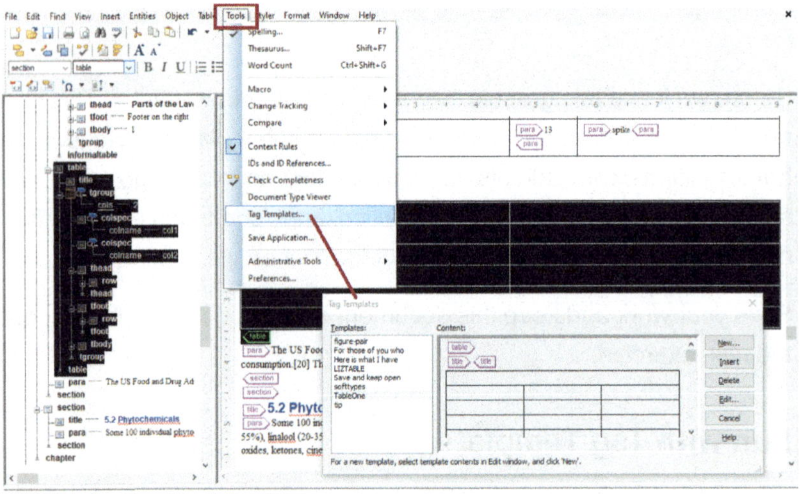

4. Select **Tag Templates** from the drop-down menu.
5. Select **New**

Fun with Tag Templates

6. Name the Tag Template and save it by clicking OK.

Figure 48. Name the Tag Template

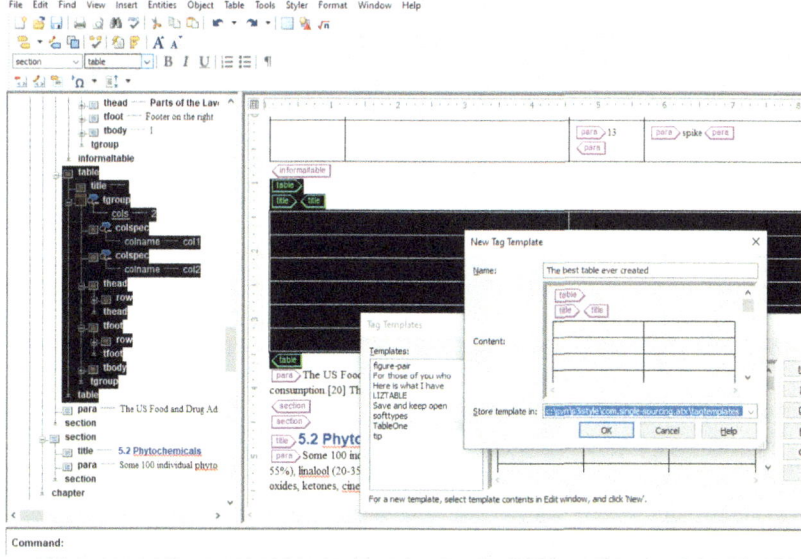

The next time you need the table, simply Insert it from the Tag Templates. Experiment with other templates.

Here is what I have:

Going forward all the Tag Templates will be available for me to use. I know this might be obvious, but your Tag Templates will be locked to the DTD you are using when you created them. So, if you created a template in DocBook, it will not work in DITA.

I delete Tag Templates after projects since their purpose ends with the project. But you can keep yours for future projects.

81

Figure 49. Tag Template ready to fill in

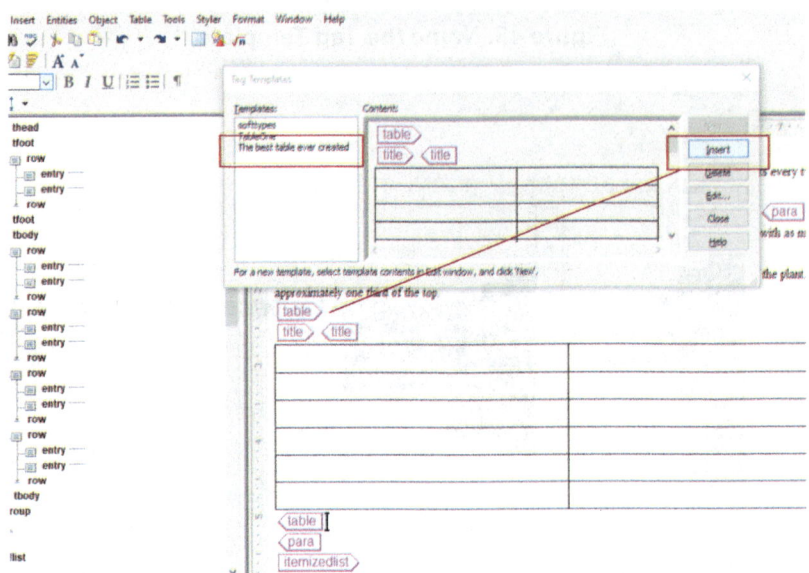

Note

You can keep the templates local to you or share them with a work team.

Save your work and keep this document open. You'll use it to work out the next exercise.

Publishing in Arbortext

Once you have entered all your content pieces into the proper elements and you've checked your markup, it's time to see the fruits of your labor. You have published before, so this is no different since we are still using the out-of-the-box style sheets.

Publishing in Arbortext

1. To Publish, go to File, and drop down the options list. Select Publish PDF.

   By now you have done this at least once before, so you are familiar with the way to initiate the publishing action.

   Figure 50. Request to publish

   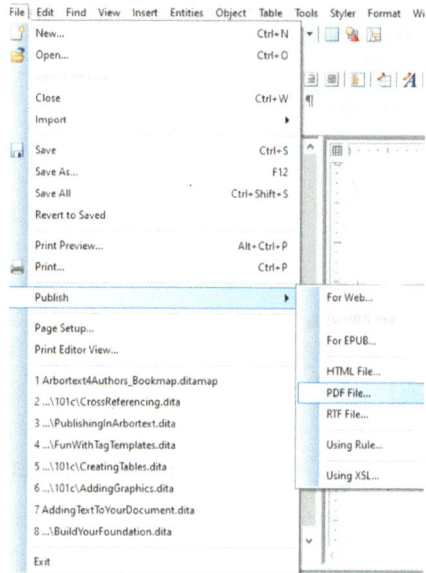

   The Output menu will appear. From here you can select the save document location (Save As) and verify the style sheet used for composition.

Figure 51. Set the Save As location and pick the style sheet

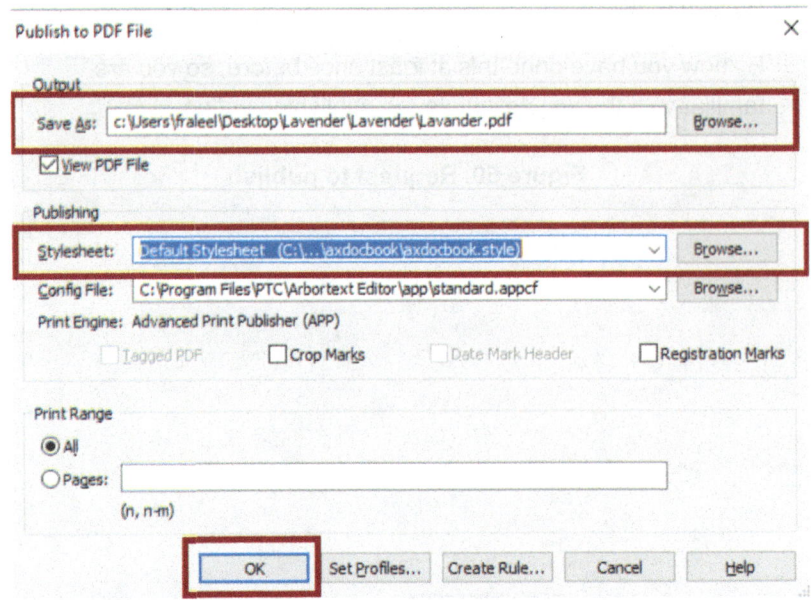

2. Simply press the Enter button. We are using the out-of-the-box style sheet so no need to change any settings here.

Here is what I have:

Here you can see the view from inside Editor next to the published output.

Cross-referencing

Figure 52. Side by side view of published output and markup

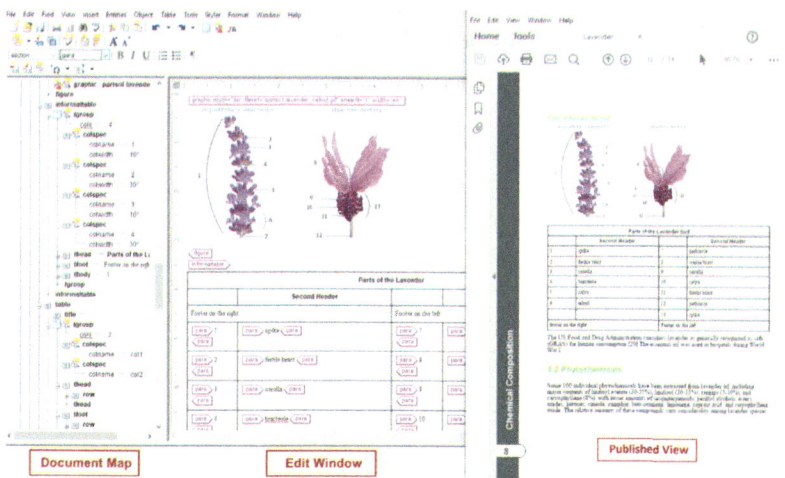

Congratulations! You have reached the finish line for creating your very first Arbortext Editor DocBook document. Save your work and keep this document to use for future practice.

Cross-referencing

In order to link, you'll need an ID to link to. Creating Linking IDs in Arbortext Editor is as simple as waving a magic wand.

Open the Attributes for the element and you'll see the ID box and a magic wand. Click on the wand and an ID is automatically generated for you. Don't worry about the ID convention, just let the tool do it for you.

CAUTION

If you try to change or delete the ID later it will break your document.

You can create an ID on any element.

1. Open the Attribute table for the element.

85

2. Find the ID field and click on the magic wand..

Figure 53. Create an ID

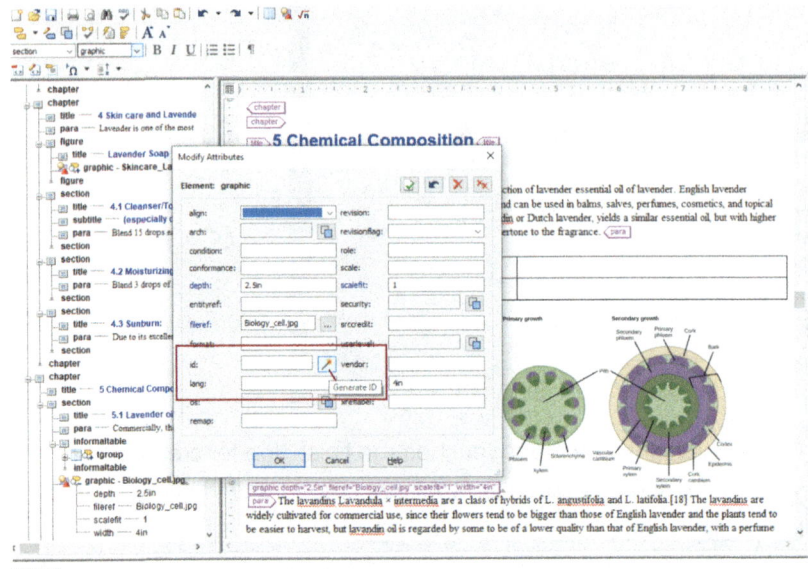

Now you have the IDREF value to connect with.

Here is what I have:

Creating ID's is so incredibly easy that is seems ridiculous to even mention it. But here you go. I created ID's at several levels. I'd also like to point out how easy it is to see the ID in the Document Map view.

Cross-referencing

Figure 54. Create ID's for many element types

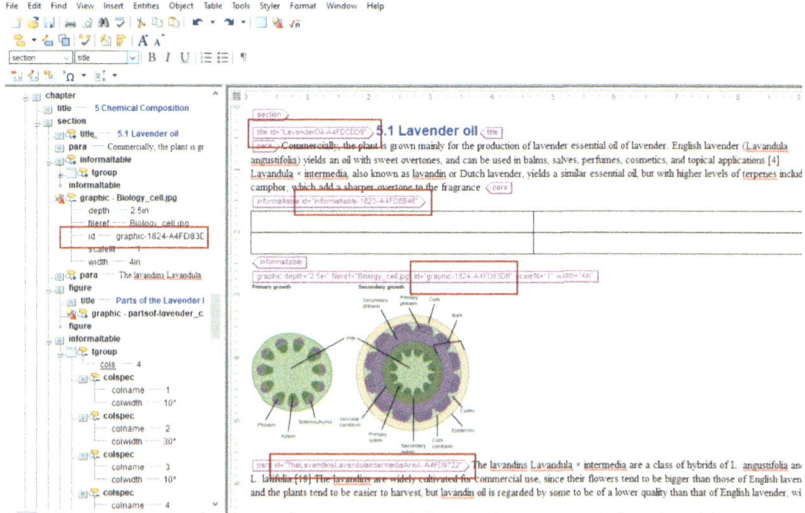

Save your work. You can go back and repeat any of the steps.

87

Chapter 7. Authoring your first DITA document in Arbortext Editor

Topics Covered in this Chapter
- DITA in 30 seconds
- All work starts with a plan
- The Resource Manager
- The DITA Map
- Create a DITA Map and then fill it in
- Special options in DITA

Traditional architecture is a top down approach and all the content is contained in one wrapper. DITA takes this all apart and looks at content in logical modules based on two things: what is the purpose or point of the information and what is the reader expecting.

DITA is an architectural model that is drastically different than any other. It was first developed by IBM and approved as an OASIS standard in 2005. At this point the architecture is well established and is widely adopted.

> **Note**
>
> Here is a bit of trivia for you: IBM used Arbortext Editor when they were developing the DITA model.

The architecture forces the writer to change the way they author. Writing for DITA topics challenges us to get rid of low value text and text that states the obvious. The idea is to use a minimal amount of text to properly inform the reader about the topic.

DITA in 30 seconds

DITA changes everything!

The magic of DITA is in the modules, or topics. The bits and pieces that come together to build the final output are the assigned order of the authored topics. The topics can be put together and shuffled depending on the content the consumer needs. Maps are what we create to compose an ordered collection of topics. DITA's topic-based approach to authoring also leads authors to write small, stand-alone modules that can readily be reused in multiple document compositions.

Reuse is at the Topic level, Block level, and Sentence level.

All content must conform into a topic type. These are the main topic types and the building blocks of your finished document: Concept, Reference, Task, Glossary, and Topic.

- **Concept** is a topic that explains or defines a thing.
- **Reference** is a topic that describes the regular features of a subject or product. Its what the reader would go to for source information.
- **Task** is a topic that covers step-by-step procedures. It's one of the easiest topics to classify.
- **Glossary** is a topic that defines a single sense of one term; not the most common topic type.
- **Topic** refers to a generic topic that should rarely be used; only for special cases.

  Note

  If you find you have way more References than Concepts, you're probably on the right path, especially if you are writing technical manuals.

DITA is widely accepted and rapidly becoming the preferred architecture. It's still evolving and there are new specializations for DITA. DITA is a much larger topic and deserves it's own attention to really master all the nuances, which is way beyond the scope of this book.

And that's DITA in 30 seconds.

A word before you move forward

Before you start building your first DITA document I want to let you know that just about every one of the lessons you learned in the previous exercises apply in DITA as well. I will point out where there may be some differences and some significant enhancements for user features. But, for the most part text is text, graphics get treated the same, tables are still tables, and the way to publish is the same.

When learning DITA in Editor all the focus should be on authoring content, not on new tool tricks. That is the point after all—to become better writers.

All work starts with a plan

Before you ever start your first DITA document, you need to establish a solid plan. And since DITA is so different in basic structure, a plan becomes tremendously beneficial for your sanity and your success.

Should you migrate or re-author

If you have finished your DocBook document, then you can simply use this document as your starting point. Depending on your style of writing, this could be fairly easy or very difficult. For legacy content projects we have often found that re-authoring is the best and most expedient course to take.

To figure that out for yourself, you can go through your newly created DocBook file and assign topics to each logical module. Don't worry about being too broad or too granular. Chances are you will change your mind once you learn more. The most important part of this is to start learning how to identify when you have a Task and when you have a Reference and just what is a Concept. Apply the basic guidelines to your content.

You may end up with a hybrid of content that will easily migrate over and other areas where you may want to re author. Sometimes you can even find this in a paragraph. I have seen several occasions when a step process was buried inside a narrative paragraph. It's easy to do; I think we have all done it at least once.

Use what ever method of documenting your analysis that works for you. I like mapping on paper or spreadsheets. The key here is to develop a solid plan to build from.

Once you have completed your analysis, building your DITA document is amazingly simple and straightforward in Arbortext.

Here is what I have:

I went through my book on lavender and I took the top level of chapters. I analyzed the chapter to see if it described one thing well or were there more than one key subjects covered. I then dissected further to see what was a Concept versus what was Reference material. I found my chapters had a combination of Concept, Reference, and sometimes a Task or two.

Once I finished analyzing my document I assigned all the content to one of these three topic types: Concept, Reference, or Task. If I ran into anything that didn't fit, I pulled it out if it offered no benefit for the reader or I classed it as content that needed to be re authored. My Tasks were very clear to see and I ended up with very few Concepts and more References. I also ended up with a list of Topic titles in the process. Once I accomplished this, I knew it was time to jump to the next step: building my DITA document.

The Resource Manager

Figure 55. Content mapped to DITA structure

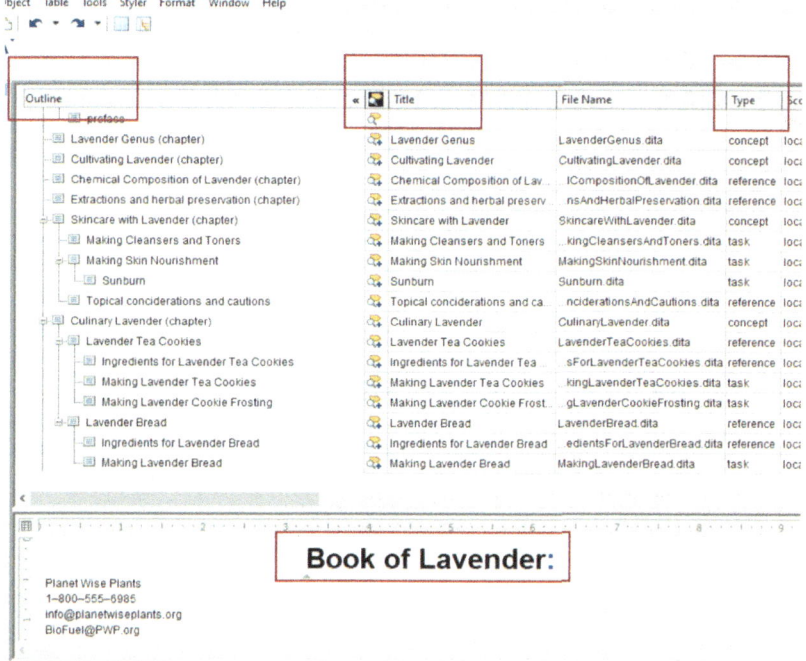

We will walk through creating the DITA Map together. This is where most of the DITA work takes place. The rest is simply doing what you already know how to do from the previous exercises. The markup may be different, but the tool still works the same.

The Resource Manager

When you choose the DITA document type in Arbortext Editor you are given a new panel in the interface. The Resource Manager does exactly what the name suggests: it allows you to manage the content that goes into your document.

One of my favorite Arbortext Editor features is the Resource Manager. It's a tool you never knew you needed and once you use it, you can't imagine getting by without it. I bring it up now since we are about to launch into DITA in Arbortext and I want you to know you have this resource at the DITA Map level as well as the Topic level.

Similar to how the Document Map gives you the aerial view of your document, the Resource Manager gives you a ready list of various content pieces and, in the case of images, the ability to preview before including them in your document. The Resource Manager is available for both the DITA Map and the Topic files.

When you are creating DITA Maps you have three tabs to use.

- Topic—If you are selecting from topics that already exist
- New Topic—Create a new topic and immediately add it to your map
- Key Definition—For inserting local or external key definitions

The Resource Manager

Figure 56. Resource Manager and Topic management

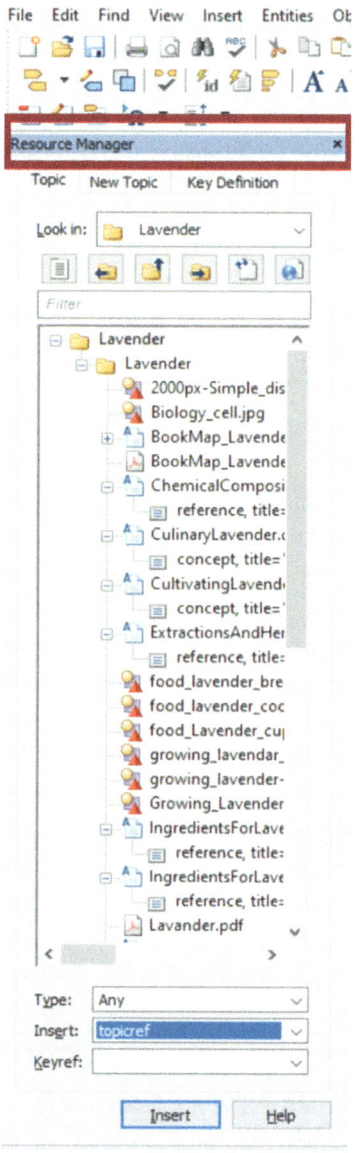

When you are inside the Topic, the options in the Resource Manager change. all the things you can do in the Topic

- Content Reference—Allows you to insert elemental content
- Link/Xref—Link or cross-reference to local or external documents
- Image—List of images in a file location and preview before adding

Figure 57. Resource Manager and Image management

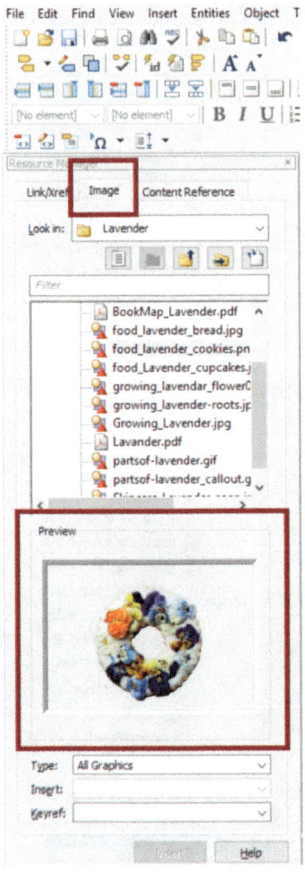

If you feel a little crowded in the application interface with three working panels open, you can either undock by double-clicking on the box title or you can close it by clicking the x next to the title. It's easy to open it again by clicking on the icon in the top tool bar or, from the **View** drop-down menu, select **Resource Manager**.

Spend a little time becoming familiar with all the options that Resource Manager gives you. It can do more than what I have mentioned. I've given you what I use the most.

The DITA Map

The DITA Map is what you will use to bring order to your documents. It is what we use to create a hierarchy when needed.

Maps are the magic that makes DITA work.

You have two types of maps to choose from in Arbortext: a Map or a BookMap. The BookMap is a template that includes the front matter and back matter you would expect for a book, whereas the Map can be used for just about everything else. Maps keep your topics organized and enforce a hierarchy where needed. You can have maps for a single use, maps for different audiences, maps for different channels, and maps for parts of a whole e.g., a chapter map that is a part of a larger book.

> **Expert tip!**
>
> When authoring DITA in Arbortext, you will get very comfortable creating maps. Maps are simply an organization of topics and a hierarchy for the topics to line up in. Treat Maps like you would a sketch pad.

Arbortext for Authoring

Figure 58. Map for generic collections and BookMap for books

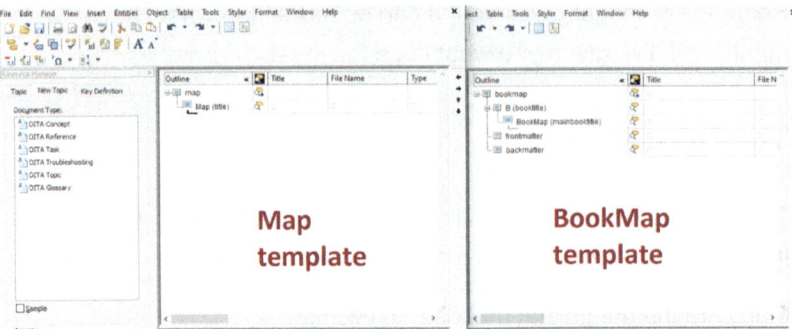

Since you've gone through and planned out your document conversion and you know what topics you need, you should be ready to map it out. So, let's go create your first DITA document in Arbortext!

Create a DITA Map and then fill it in

A DITA Map is our starting place when creating new documents in Arbortext.

You've developed a plan and gathered the content pieces, it is time to outline your project as we did in the DocBook exercise. In DITA we start with a map to help us create the rough structure for the final publication. Since you just went through all of this with your DocBook document you should be ready to go. Keep in mind the DITA requires that the content fits into the topic types.

> **Expert tip!**
>
> Taking your last project and reauthoring it in DITA might be very insightful for you. You may discover what most people encounter—the value of rewriting content for DITA rather than trying to simply copy it over.

Starting a new map is just like starting all other new files you have already done. Once you open the new map, name it, and save it. to your Playground folder.

Create a DITA Map and then fill it in

Note

You can either create a DITA Map or a DITA Bookmap. The Bookmap will give you the frontmatter and backmatter you would need for a proper book publication. Maps are easy to create and can be discarded and recreated depending on your needs.

1. Where your cursor is matters. So, make sure you are where you want your topic to be. You can move topics later if you want to rearrange.

Figure 59. Create the New Topic

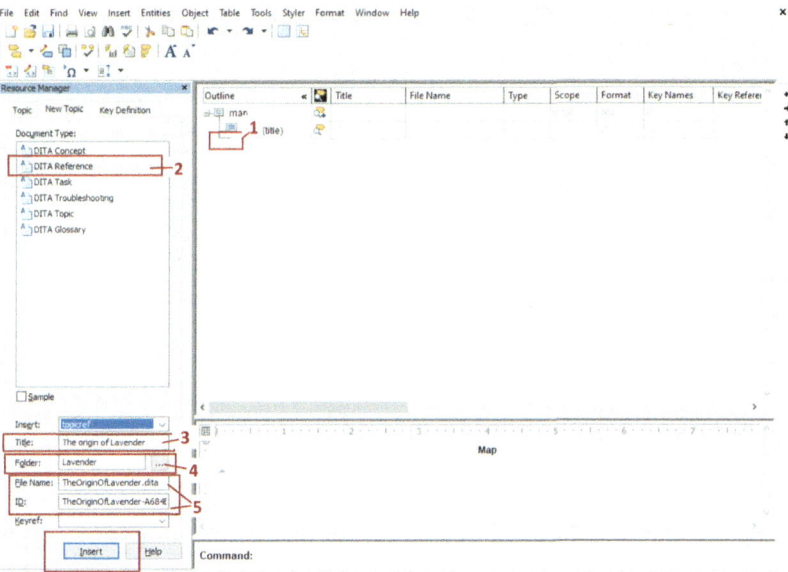

2. Pick a new topic type or browse topics in a file if you have already created them.

   Note

   To determine which type of topic you need, consider the purpose it serves the reader and content contained. Once you pick a topic type, you cannot simply change the topic type if you change your mind later.

3. Creating a new topic is very easy, simply type the title for the topic.
4. Assign the location where your topics will be stored.
5. As you type the title, the file name and ID are automatically filled in for you. Press Insert and this will create your topic and place it into the Map.

   Note

   You can always change the order of the Topics by grabbing and dragging them up or down. You can also change the level. But if you change your mind about the topic type, you have to rewrite it.

Here is what I have:

I built my map, opened all my topics, added all my content pieces. Now all I need to do is publish!

Create a DITA Map and then fill it in

Figure 60. My DITA Map example

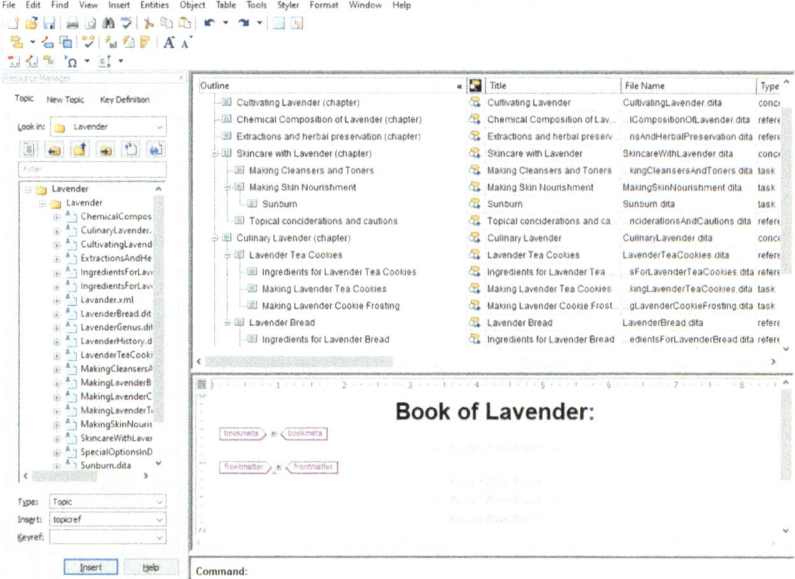

Save your work. You can go back and repeat any of the steps or simply publish.

Authoring your topics

Using the content that you gathered and the content you will convert from your last exercise, fill in the details for your topics.

Use the map you just created to help guide you through adding content—text, images, tables, and lists—to build out your topic.

1. Select the topic title from the map you wish to open.

Arbortext for Authoring

2. Open the topic.

- Right-click your mouse to pull up the Menu and select **Open** {topictitle}.

- From the File drop-down menu, select **Open** {topictitle}

Figure 61. Opening topics

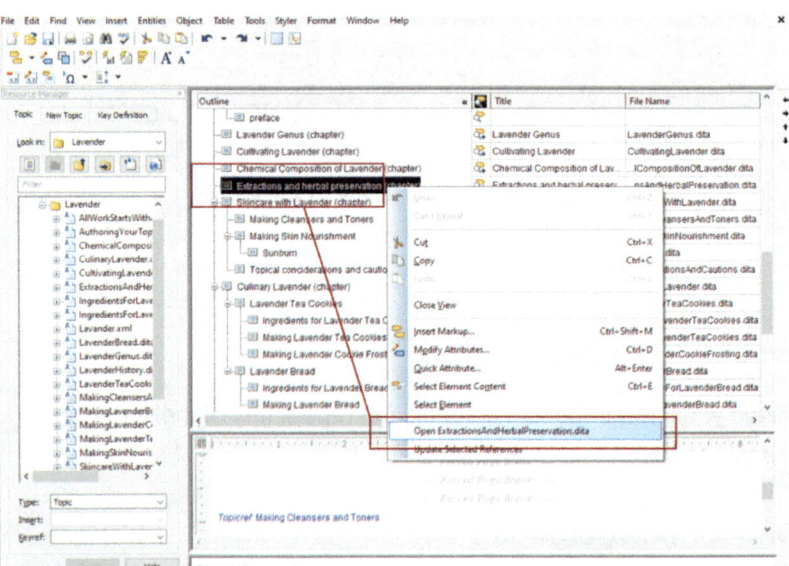

3. Once opened, edit just like you edit any other document. The practice is the same as building the DocBook file, only the markup has changed—text, images, and tables.

4. Repeat steps one, two, and three through every topic then you will have a full DITA document.

Congratulations! You are ready to publish.

Here is what I have:

I used the standard DITA style sheet that comes out of the box. You can see the style sheet has formatted the document and I have page

Special options in DITA

numbers, chapter numbers, alignment, and you can see the special formatting for at least two title types.

Figure 62. Sample Published page

Special options in DITA

For the most part, Editor is Editor. Because of its robustness, no matter what standard you are authoring to, Editor can handle it.

In case you hadn't noticed, DITA offers some simplifications when it comes to markup. Did you notice the significantly shorter list of allowed elements when you were authoring? But along with the minimizing of elements, there are some differences and some new elements offered with DITA that help simplify and automate the authoring process.

These are some of my favorites.

Lists

DITA introduces a couple of new element options when it comes to lists. You'll still have the ordered list and the unordered list.

The first new list is <dl>—Definition List—which gives you the option to create and format a list of terms and the corresponding definition. With Arbortext, when you use the< dl> markup, a predesignated table is also inserted. All you need to do is fill in the blank. The table also has options for formatting, and you can pull them up the same way you would any other table.

Term heading	Description heading

Sure, I could manually build this with the DITA standard elements, but it's so nice to have this configured for me.

The other new list option that is a part of the DITA standard is <sl>—the Simple List—which gives you the ability to have a list with no bullets. The items should all be short and can be phrases but are short enough to fit on one line. For example, a list of ingredients works well:

> 1 tablespoon culinary lavender flowers, dried
>
> 1 cup butter, room temperature
>
> 2/3 cup granulated sugar
>
> 1 teaspoon pure vanilla extract
>
> 1/4 teaspoon lemon extract
>
> 2 cups all-purpose flour
>
> 1/8 teaspoon salt

Tables

Arbortext Editor supports standard tables and custom tables declared in a DTD. It always has and DITA is no different. But what is different in DITA is the number of elements that are a table. There are two elements: <table> and <simpletable>. How easy is that?!

If you want a Titled Numbered Table that shows on a List of Tables, it's simple to just add the <title> markup inside the table.

Just a table

A listed table with a title

Table 3. Now I have a numbered table

Then there is the simple table

Of course, we still have the simple table perfect for tabular lists of all sorts. There isn't much formatting needed or required when it comes to simple tabular lists.

Simple tables don't have titles

Column 1 heading	Column 2 heading

Graphics

There really is no difference in graphics or images beyond some nuance changes in markup language.

When I use the <fig> element. I have a list of other formatting options I can include inside that element. A title is no longer required and what was called informal table (informaltable) in DocBook is now a simple table that comes with a header row already assigned and an assumption you will want to title the columns.

Image with a title and a legend table

Figure 63. Parts of the lavender bud

Column 1 heading	Column 2 heading

Special options in DITA

You can change the formatting if you want to get rid of the header row. Inserting an image is just like with DocBook and many other specs out there.

Just an image

Inline image

An inline image is a graphic that appears inline in the middle of the sentence.

107

Chapter 8. Best practices for all authors

We have an advantage coming from a consulting perspective as well as being very active in the Tech Comm community at large. We get to find out what everybody is doing. People share their candid views on business practices and share what worked and what did not. As a result, we have found some universal practices that are very beneficial for those who use them.

The guides every author needs

Before you begin to write, you should have the specifications of the architecture you will be authoring in. Whether you are authoring in MIL-STD or DITA or DocBook, or some other proprietary structure, you should have access to documentation about the rules.

Style guides help explain the way the content will be presented after composition. This is automated by the publishing engine, but it helps authors to understand what the decisions are and how their markup is handled.

Authoring guides give you particulars about the specific markup to be used and why.

I always find it odd, but not unusual, when a group of communicators don't have the key communication tools for themselves. Besides not making one, the biggest mistake people tend to make with guides is in treating them as if they were steadfast. You should have a regular practice of reviewing and revising your guides. Keep them relevant for your company and for the changing authoring practices.

Plan it out

How does that saying go?

"If you fail to plan, you are planning to fail."

—Benjamin Franklin

It is important to take a moment to create a plan. It doesn't have to be the best plan and it doesn't mean you have to strictly stick to it. You can adapt and change as the need demands but take the little bit of front-end effort to develop the best plan you can

Use it or lose it

With Arbortext, every time you open a new file it comes with a preset of elements. You don't necessarily need to use all of them. For the ones you won't use, delete them. Keep it clean.

This is also a good exercise for learning to be a minimalist author. Write then read it back. Remove low-value content and re-read. If the message is still clear then you can lose it. If the message is not clear then your reader needs to use it, so put it back.

Know your exit before you take off

Nothing ever stays the same. We like to think it does, but business is not static. Architectures change over time, so you want to be able to adapt too. While it may be impossible to predict the future with any certainty, you can still prepare now.

First, be aware that the design choices you make today will impact the future. For example; you don't have to be in DITA to begin practicing some of the basic tenets of minimalism and omitting low-value content. Adopt authoring practices that keep an eye out for reuse whenever possible. Does your content have modules that can stand alone?

Second, have an exit plan or at least know ahead of time what it will take to get out. You may be on one path today and that path may be just fine, but you may want to change paths in the future. For example, you may be in unstructured authoring now, but you may be moving to DITA in the next year. Is there a transition step between here and there? How would you move out of this transition into the end goal? What if you wanted—or needed—to change from DITA to something else?

There is a cost for everything. We need to walk into the future with our eyes wide open and aware of what the costs are beforehand.

Get involved

Don't sit on the sidelines. Get involved with the community and engage with your peers. There is nothing like shared wisdom and the writers' community is a very active and communicative group. I have had the privilege of being introduced to this community from the very beginning and I am always impressed. For a group of introverts, they are the most outgoing and sharing group of professionals I have had the privilege to meet. We all learn from each other, inspire each other, and support each other. So, jump in, the water is warm!

Chapter 9. Top Arbortext and authoring resources

Authoring resources

The best way to learn is tribal so I highly recommend that you get involved with one of the membership groups serving the Tech Comm profession.

STC — Society for Technical Communication has a very active national community and a growing international one.

AMWA — American Medical Writers Association is for the medical writers.

S3I — Single-Sourcing Solutions hosts a community-driven web series that meets every month. You can visit our website for more information.

Read up on the topics you need to gain a deeper understanding in. There are many books that go into detail about writing techniques and best practices. Single-Sourcing Solutions has a good list we make available to our Affinity Group members in addition to the other important resources.

Arbortext resources

Help from inside the tool—Every good tool maker wants you to be successful. Arbortext Editor has an extensive help menu. They also have some tutorials you can use to help deepen your knowledge.

PTC Community—PTC has a community page dedicated to all things Arbortext. You can find updates on what is going on with the product suite, questions from other users and answers, and some tips. The developers keep an eye on this page, so we strongly encourage you to let your voice be heard here.

Arbortext for Authoring

Single-Sourcing Solutions—There is a monthly Affinity Group group meeting dedicated to Arbortext and one for Windchill, the content management solution. And, in case you did not know, we wrote the books on Arbortext. You can find them on the Single-Sourcing Solutions website. www.single-sourcing.com

Afterword

Thanks for reading!

If you enjoyed it, you might be ready to advance to *Arbortext 102*. It's all about how to create multi-channel stylesheets for Arbortext publishing.

Join our mailing list to get tips every month and get notified when our next books are ready: mailinglist.single-sourcing.com

Everyone at Single-Sourcing Solutions participates in community projects—and we have a lot of them! To take advantage of one of our public service projects, go to social.single-sourcing.com and pick the one that works best for you.

You can always reach us directly, too. Email us at info@single-sourcing.com. We're here to help.

Index

A

add comments 59
address element 11
AMWA 113
Arbortext
 compared with other tools ... 23
 end-to-end solution, *See*
  Arbortext Product Suite
 installation 3
*Arbortext 101: Best
Practices for Configuring,
Authoring, Styling, and
Publishing with Arbortext* 3
Arbortext Editor 1, 13, 23, 27–28, 67, 89
Arbortext eLearning Library 1
Arbortext IsoDraw 13
Arbortext Product Suite 13
Arbortext Publishing Engine ... 13
Arbortext Styler 13
attributes 11
authoring tool, *See* Arbortext
 Editor

B

benefits of structured
 authoring 5
blockquote element 11
bold 11
 See also attributes

C

calling entities 11
chapter element 37
citation element 11
collapsing and expanding
 elements in map view 56
colspec element 73
colwidth element 73
comments
 inserting 59
company entity 11
content management tool, *See*
 Windchill
content repository, *See* Windchill
copyright entity 11
create DITA topic 93, 98
 See also Resource
  Manager
create new document
 free-form 38
 planning 61, 91
create pdf, *See* publish pdf
creating content 91
Creo Illustrate 13
cursor location 27, 67

D

declaring entities 11
decrease font size icon 34
descriptive writing 5

DITA 1, 8, 45, 61, 64, 89, 91, 93, 97–98, 101, 103, 109
    graphics 103
    lists 103
    maps and bookmaps ... 97–98, 101
    open topic from map 101
    tables 103
    topic types 89, 91
dl element 103
DocBook 8, 45, 61, 64, 109
doctype, *See* DTD
document map view ... 30, 53, 67
    expanding and collapsing ... 56
    See also moving elements
document type, *See* DTD
Document Type Definition, *See* DTD
DTD 8, 37
    See also custom doctype
    See also DITA
    See also DocBook
    See also MIL-STD

E

elements
    moving or rearranging 53
emphasis element 11
entities 11
    about 11
    calling 11
    declaring 11

example element 11
expanding and collapsing elements in map view 56

F

fig element 103
figure element 11
fix table cell size 73
font size
    icons 34
    increasing or decreasing size on screen 34
formatting tables 73

G

graphics 93
    See also Resource Manager
    adding 69
    inserting 69
    modifying attributes 69
    sizing and scaling 69
greyed out navigation item 28

I

IBM 8
illustration tool, *See* Arbortext IsoDraw
image element 103
img element 11
increase font size icon 34

Index

informaltable element 73
inserting comments 59
italics 11
   See also attributes

K

keyboard shortcuts 23, 28, 45, 53, 59

L

learning resources 113
licensing
   trial licenses 3

M

markup
   Add Markup Window ... 38, 45, 67
   adding 38, 45, 67
   Change Markup Window 51
   changing 51
   deleting 51
   from navigation menu .. 38, 45, 51, 67
markup language 11, 38
   See also markup
migrating content 91
MIL-STD 8, 64, 109
moving elements 53

N

navigating in documents 56
new sample document 29
note element 11

P

para element 37
paragraph element 51
planning your work 61, 64, 89, 91, 109
playground
   setting up 25, 98
plus icon 69
preferences, *See* user preferences
procedural writing 5
PTC Communities 113
publish dialog window 38, 82
publish document 38, 82
publish pdf 38, 82

R

remark element 51
REMOVE structured authoring
   benefits 5
   how it works 5
   reuse 5
Resource Manager 93
   See also DITA
   graphics 93
   resources 113

119

See also community

reuse 91
   content 91

S

sample document 29
saving published output 82
section element 11, 37
set up playground 25, 98
SGML 11, 13
shortcuts, *See* keyboard shortcuts
simpletable element 103
sl element 103
splitting the view pane 30
STC 113
structured authoring 5
Structured Generalized Markup Language, *See* SGML
style guides 109
styling tool, *See* Arbortext Styler

T

table element 11, 73, 103
tables 73
tag
   about 37
   moving, *See* moving elements
   open and closing 37
tag display 31
tag templates 79
TC Dojo 113

tgroup element 73
title element 5, 45, 103
toolbars 28
trial licenses 3
tutorials 113

U

underline 11
   See also attributes
user interface 23
user preferences
   changing 33

V

valid XML 37, 45
view, *See* tag display

W

well-formed XML 37–38
Windchill 13
   content management 13
window view
   document map view 30, 53
   edit view 53, 67
   font size on screen 34
   split view 30
writer entity 11
WYSIWYG 5

X

XML 13
XML publishing 5
XML Schema Definition
  (XSD) 8

Made in the USA
Coppell, TX
20 December 2024

43273476R00075